NORTH BAY
FARMERS MARKETS
COOKBOOK

D1275245

NORTH BAY
FARMERS MARKETS
COOKBOOK

BRIGITTE MORAN
WITH AMELIA SPILGER

Photographs by Scott Ellison

GIBBS SMITH
TO ENRICH AND INSPIRE HUMANKIND
Salt Lake City | Charleston | Santa Fe | Santa Barbara

First Edition
13 12 11 10 09   5 4 3 2 1

Published by
Gibbs Smith
P.O. Box 667
Layton, Utah 84041

Orders: 1.800.835.4993
www.gibbs-smith.com

Printed and bound in China
Gibbs Smith books are printed on either recycled, 100% post-consumer waste, FSC-certified papers,
or on paper produced from a 100% certified sustainable forest/controlled wood source.

Library of Congress Cataloging-in-Publication Data
Moran, Brigitte.
  North Bay farmers markets cookbook / Brigitte Moran with Amelia Spilger ; photographs by Scott
Ellison. — 1st ed.
      p. cm.
  Includes bibliographical references and index.
  ISBN-13: 978-1-4236-0313-9
  ISBN-10: 1-4236-0313-3
  1. Natural foods—California. 2. Cookery. 3. Moran, Brigitte. I. Spilger, Amelia. II. Title.
TX369.M65 2009
  641.5'63609794—dc22
                                         2008050428

This cookbook is dedicated to my family, friends, local community, and all the farmers, bakers, and candlestick makers for whom I work. Thank you for your support.

CONTENTS

INTRODUCTION
A FRENCH-AMERICAN PARADOX

I have been eating for fifty-one years. My story as an eater has had many influences, beginning with my lessons in what to eat from my French parents and their deeply rooted food traditions that blended the north and south of France. My years as a teenage eater in the late '60s and early '70s paralleled the coming of age of overly processed industrialized food in America. Then came my experience as a young naïve mother teaching my twin daughters and my son what is good to eat. And finally, my relationship with food has been influenced by twenty years of facilitating farmers markets and cherishing the feeling of being deeply connected to my community, the land, and the people who grow my food. This is just one story, but encompassed in my history as an eater are the stories of thousands of eaters, eaters who feel they have lost their traditions surrounding food, eaters who have felt misled by the industrial food pyramid, and eaters who are hungry for a sense of connection to a local, healthy food system.

If I were just French, this would be simple. I would savor rich pâtés, fresh butter croissants, crusted baguettes with assorted cheeses, and a daily glass of red wine. I would be guiltless and thin, and you would despise me. If only I were just French.

Fortunately, for the purposes of this book, I have a more layered story to share. I am French/ Canadian/American. My family immigrated to Marin County, California, in 1961, drawn by promises of the American Dream. My *maman*, Annick, was a stunning Gaelic-looking French woman with jet black hair, green eyes, and a taste for fish, crêpes, and other light foods typical of northern France. My papa, Charles, with his dark skin and chiseled features resembled James Dean and preferred heavy meats, sausages, and the signature cheeses of southern France. With three children and little to no English-speaking skills, they pursued an uncharted path thousands of miles from our family's roots and brought French food traditions along with them for comfort.

When I started school at age five, I was the chubby French girl with a pixie who didn't speak much English and ate weird French food. My lunch consisted of baguettes with *real* butter and a French chocolate bar. Afternoon snacks included homemade French fries, charcuterie plates, and Brie cheese. Instead of Tollhouse chocolate chip cookies, my mother made homemade crêpes with nutella and dished up creative concoctions from yesterday's leftovers. You can imagine my classmates' fascination.

My mother, like any decent French woman of her time, had learned to prepare traditional French meals from scratch. She cooked from memory or with guidance from the meticulously handwritten book of recipes she carried with her since her days in Riantec,

France, in the Province of Brittany. There she had embarked on her secondary education in cooking and sewing along with other French mademoiselles who were not pursuing professional degrees. Masterfully sharing her culture's food traditions with her family and friends was to be an honorable and celebrated part of her life's work.

Even with this strong French base, after a few years living in the States, our French food traditions began to evolve and eventually dissolve, acquiescing to the dominant food culture that surrounded us. My mother, who had been steeped in a food tradition based on whole ingredients, fresh produce, and homemade everything, abandoned much of her heritage for the convenience of Ragu, Tang, and Space Sticks—"the healthy food for astronauts." Taste was not the appeal of prepackaged foods; rather it was the novelty that something could be so easy and so fast. It was progress. It was, well, American.

We weren't the only family allowing our traditions to fall by the wayside. It was a common trend for many reasons. With so many immigrant families coming to the United States, especially post–WWII refugees, there were thousands of food cultures bumping up against one another—cross-pollination was inevitable. In the fields, food production in America was becoming much more "efficient," as large industrialized farms, armed with the chemical pesticides and fertilizers of the Green Revolution, overtook small family farms. They were cheered on from the sidelines by USDA's secretary Ezra Taft Benson (1953–61) and Earl Butz (1971–76), shouting "get big, or get out," plant commodity crops "fence row to fence row," and "adapt or die."[1] Food manufacturers capitalized on the new abundance of commodity crops by crafting foodlike substances and employing their skilled marketing teams to convince eaters that inside every box was the most innovative new spin on the same list of ingredients: corn, wheat, soybeans, rice, and all their derivatives. At the same time, a growing feminist movement was liberating women from the kitchens. Prepackaged fast food allowed the pace of their lives to keep up with the pace of progress and corporate America, without missing a beat on the home front. This new food culture was a powerful wave; composed of compounding currents that swept us all away, including the newest arrivals to America, like our impressionable French family.

In the late 1970s, that same little girl with a pixie haircut married a sixth-generation Californian. I became a mother of three, kicking it off with a set of twins when I was twenty-one years old. Our meals were a fusion, or rather a collision, of food cultures. I grew up on pâté, whereas my husband, Herb, grew up on meatloaf. While I was accustomed to French chocolate and butter, he ate Hershey's milk chocolate and drank Coca-Cola. In our adulthood, we both let go of Space Sticks, thank goodness, but other staples of the culture of convenience had a stronghold on our pantry.

We raised our family at the height of the convenient food–boom, and to be honest, I was thankful for it at the time. Life was busy, and I got lazy when it came to cooking; juggling three young children, working multiple jobs, and going to school left little time for making homemade stews. Frozen ready-to-eat foods were luxurious quick fixes. McDonald's, with their seemingly balanced Happy Meal, complete with a toy that I could use as leverage, didn't seem that bad. I put my trust in the USDA and didn't spend too much time questioning the hormones in our milk or the antibiotics in our beef. The marketing got me. I wanted to believe that the Photoshopped picture of a perfectly ripe red tomato would taste like the tomatoes I remembered from trips to my Grandmere's garden in France. When they didn't, my initial disappointment was followed by the thought, "Well, they just don't make them like they used to," not the realization that the system itself was flawed.

In 1989, my best friend, Patti, and I started the Downtown Farmers Market in San Rafael. It was designed to be a vibrant community gathering place and has thrived in that role for the last twenty years. While life was still busy and convenient food still had its appeal, Thursday evenings at the farmers market helped keep our families grounded by providing a weekly connection to farmers and to our community. Until recently, the majority of people who came to the market weren't thinking about the benefits of local, seasonal, or organic food. Terms like sustainable agriculture, locavore, food shed, and ecological footprint were yet to be coined. Still, people gravitated to the market, following their instincts that fresh local food available in a dynamic community setting had to be a good thing.

What began as a defiant undercurrent

of long-haired hippy farmers (I can say that because I count some of the most revolutionary ones as my friends) has now flooded mainstream culture with heightened consciousness about the hard-to-stomach realities of our industrialized food system. It has always fascinated me that although my parents' generation generally viewed the "hippy" movement as one of radicals, those back-to-the-land hippies were merely trying to reclaim a simpler lifestyle and a more healthful and transparent food system reminiscent of past generations. My parents and grandparents had more in common with hippy farmers than I think they'd like to admit.

As the road from farm to fork becomes more transparent, eaters are finding their voice and beginning to demand food that takes into account the health of the consumer, the farmer, and the land. We are relearning how to decipher what is good to eat, shedding decades of USDA food pyramids and savvy marketing ploys that have only served to confuse the eater.

While I have always been aware of the benefit of bringing the community together around good food, I have only recently begun to understand the complexities of the system that brings us our food. I believe that we're all works in progress. For example, just in the last two years, I've switched to organic milk, given up Diet Coke, and started bringing my own mug to Starbucks. Yes, I'm a regular at my local Starbucks. To those who drink raw organic milk, who would never dream of consuming artificial sugars, and who frequent mom-and-pop coffee shops exclusively, these changes to my daily habits may not seem like much. But I'd argue that we're all at different places on our paths and that condemnation is no way to bring someone along. I think the best way to share your values is to live them with passion and joy because that type of energy is positive and contagious.

I hope that this cookbook will convey my ever-growing passion for sustainable, local food systems. My lifetime of fifty-plus years has marked some of the most productive and destructive years in our agricultural history. The consequences are discouraging at best, but it's not too late to turn this bus around. My connection to local farmers and specialty food purveyors has been more than a nice release; it has reinvigorated my confidence that our local farmers can grow delicious, healthy, and life-nourishing foods, and has given me hope that transparent and vibrant food systems supported by committed eaters can weather whatever challenges we will face in the future. A friend once said, "If there's only one thing I'm certain of when it comes to the future, it's that we'll need a farmer three times a day." Here's to all the farmers, especially to those who inspire me every day.

THE HISTORY OF FARMERS MARKETS IN CALIFORNIA

A LOCAL MOVEMENT

A delicious revolution is gaining momentum across the United States. It's fueled by eaters who are hungry for real food and for a sense of connection to the land and the farmers who grow it. The people of the movement are diverse, ranging from the small organic farmer who has been growing food for his community for more than thirty years, to the suburban mother of three who chooses to invest in fresh local food as her family's health insurance, to the urban teenager who, while learning how to grow food in a community garden, is inspired to make healthy food choices. The movement has captured the support of environmentalists, foodies, human rights activists, parents, and politicians alike, largely because they all share one thing in common—they eat.

ED GROWS IT, ED SELLS IT. ANY QUESTIONS?

It's as simple as that when you shop at a certified farmers market. Welcome to home-grown community gathering places, where

Retired engineer-gone-farmer, Ed Pearson grows in Novato, California.

local, seasonal, fresh, flavorful, and nutrient-dense food with an ethical edge is sold direct from producer to consumer. In contrast to an industrialized food system that has masterfully confused its eaters, farmers markets are a return to delectable simplicity. While shopping at a supermarket is yet another chore on the never-ending list of things to do, the experience of shopping at a farmers market has become a cherished ritual for eaters across the nation.

The roots of the real food movement are grounded in the farmers market communities that are flourishing across this country. While the movement feels unified in its mission, the rules and regulations that govern farmers markets vary from state to state. California's vibrant farmers market community is a product of two state policies—the first threatened the viability of small family farms and the second ensured their survival.

In 1915, as California was becoming a leading exporter of agricultural products, both nationally and internationally, the California Department of Food and Agriculture created a standardization program to ensure that products would arrive at their destinations in excellent condition. Standardization laws, better known as "standard pack," established minimum standards for maturity, quality, size, standard container and pack, and container markings.

While these regulations strengthened the state's agricultural export business, standard pack severely restricted the ability of many small family farms to sell their products. Imagine being told, "Yes, your peaches are beautiful, flavorful, and mouthwatering, but you can't sell them because they're not all the same size and don't fit in this particular container." It simply wasn't cost effective for small-scale growers who were looking to sell a wide variety of products to abide by the same rules as the larger growers who were shipping pallets of one particular crop across the country.

By the mid-1970s, California had lost so many small family farms at such an alarming rate that the state assembly was called to take action. In 1977, the Farmer to Consumer Direct Marketing Act was passed. Its purpose, as hinted at by its title, was to develop and expand the direct marketing opportunities of agricultural products from farmer to consumer. Its ultimate goals were to support the economic viability of farmers and to increase consumer access to quality food. This was the beginning of farmers markets in California as we know them today.

In California, Certified Farmers Markets (CFMs) are locations approved by the county agricultural commissioner where certified farmers sell only those agricultural products they grow themselves. While farmers markets in many states strive to ensure that the sellers are authentic farmers, California is unique in that the combination of standard pack and the subsequent Direct Marketing Act serve to guarantee that California farmers markets host farmers who truly grow what they're selling.

In 1976, there was only a handful of Certified Farmers Markets in California. When we opened the Downtown Farmers Market in San Rafael twenty years ago, there were only sixty markets in the state. As of 2009, there are more than five hundred farmers markets across the state and more than 4,500 nationwide. I believe that the farmers market boom has been both the catalyst and the consequence of American consumers demanding a more transparent food system, one that is more environmentally sound, more socially just, and, more than anything else, one that simply tastes better.

At first glance, the growing number of farmers markets looks like cause for celebration. After all, what could possibly be the downside of bringing fresh local produce directly to communities nearly every day of the week? Two little words: farmer burnout. While it's charming to walk to your own neighborhood market, it's important to recognize that having multiple markets on the same day within miles of one another overextends the farmers and dilutes the customer base. In the midst of this boon, it's

MALT shopper in front of Mr. Lee and his strawberries.

important to be sensitive to the needs of the farmers and the customers.

GOOD FOR THE FARMER

Farmers markets support the economic viability of small family farms. Consider the dollar you spend at a supermarket verses the dollar you spend at the farmers market. In 2002, the USDA estimated that nineteen cents of one dollar spent at a supermarket made its way back to the farmer. (It was considerably less for products like wheat, for which only six cents landed in the farmer's pocket.) The other eighty-one cents was divvied up among the gang of middlemen that move that product from farm to processing plant, to shipping facility, to marketing table, to distribution hub, to supermarket display.

In this industrialized system, we pay considerably more for the transport of our food than for its growth, a reality that depreciates the value of farmers and the time they invest in growing our food. With only nineteen cents of your dollar making its way back to the farm, it's impossible not to wonder, "How do they grow food so cheaply? Who is paying for the environmental consequences of industrialized monocultures? Who funds the farm subsidies that keep these industrialized farms afloat?" We don't have to look too far to see who bears the burden of these hidden costs of an industrialized food system. We do.

Now consider the dollar you spend at a farmers market. Other than the nominal fee that the farmer pays for his or her stall space and the cost of gas for the farmer to come to market, your dollar goes directly into the pocket of the producer. This profit margin is pivotal to maintaining a healthy local food system so that family farms can afford to keep local land in agricultural production. In the

Russ Sartori, multi-generational dairyman, diversifies with organic strawberries.

words of Russ Sartori, a forth-generation Marin dairyman turned organic strawberry grower, "It's nice being the store for the day."

There are many ways in which Certified Farmers Markets enable small family farms to not just survive but to thrive. Sartori is a prime example of how farmers markets support the development of niche markets and serve to incubate new businesses. The farmers market is both a dynamic and a flexible venue where farmers can experiment and get direct feedback from consumers on their product, therefore building a business around the niche opportunities that present themselves. Seeing the high demand for strawberries at his local farmers markets, paired with consumer interest in food grown as close to home as possible, Sartori decided to give strawberries a go. Seven years later, his business is still going strong and his strawberries are renowned among local eaters.

GOOD FOR THE EATER

The experience of exploring rows of fresh fruits and vegetables, honey, nuts, and flowers, visiting stands with grass-fed meats, farmstead cheeses, and brick-oven breads, and all the while absorbing the stories of the people who have produced this abundance, spoils us for any other shopping venue and understandably so. Supermarket chains and mom-and-pop grocery stores across the nation, hip to the fresh and local food craze, are determined to re-create the farmers market experience. And while some do a good job of walking the talk and sourcing from local growers, none can embody the authentic experience of shopping at a farmers market.

The initial hook for most eaters is flavor. Food sold at the farmers market is allowed to ripen naturally, is picked at its prime, and usually arrives at the market within a day, sometimes within hours, of being harvested.

Fresh seasonal produce reminds us of what fruits and vegetables aspire to be. I have a girlfriend who swore for years that she didn't like tomatoes, because in her experience they were flavorless, mealy, and hard. It took one visit to the farmers market in the middle of August to change her mind. Now, you name the variety—Brandywine, Cherokee, Zebra—and she craves it. Imagine the void in her eating experience if she had continued to assume that imported tomatoes, ripened in transit, were all that nature had to offer.

Digging a little deeper, Certified Farmers Markets play a pivotal role in creating diverse, secure, and healthy food systems. Consumers now have the good fortune of being presented with an important alternative to the industrialized food system—just think, between 1915 and 1976 in California, we didn't really have a choice. Furthermore, farmers markets shrink our dependency on global trading markets, and therefore shrink our ecological footprints by shortening the distance our food travels. Not only does food taste better when it hasn't traveled thousands of miles to reach our plate, it also requires less energy in transport, resulting in a feel-good experience for any eco-conscious consumer.

EATER, MEET YOUR FARMER

One of the most unique and enticing elements of Certified Farmers Markets is the opportunity

A THRIVING PARTNERSHIP
RUSS SARTORI AND RAFAEL GUZMAN OF SARTORI FARMS IN TOMALES

For almost a century, starting in the early 1900s, Sartori's family owned and operated a dairy in Marin County. After selling the dairy in 1990, Russ Sartori partnered with Marin Agricultural Land Trust (MALT) to put an agricultural conservation easement on their 646 acres in Tomales. Shortly thereafter, in 2001, Russ embarked on the adventure of growing organic strawberries with his one full-time employee Rafael Guzman. Russ's decision to MALT his land was motivated by his desire to secure the farm for agriculture and for his kids: "I never wanted to sell or develop this land. If my kids want to farm it or sell it, it's up to them. But it's protected now, it will always be preserved as farmland."

Since its founding in 1980 to the spring of 2008, MALT has protected more than forty thousand acres of farmland in Marin County, including sixty-two family farms and ranches— land that might have been otherwise developed. MALT has certainly solved one piece of the puzzle of keeping small farms and ranches alive near a big urban city. (Photograph by Curtis Myers.)

SIMPLY THE BEST
EDDIE CHAVEZ OF EGB FARM

Eddie has been attending the farmers markets in the Bay Area for twenty-five years. He grows an assortment of stone fruits, apples, and almonds on 188 acres in Fresno. He sells both at farmers markets and wholesale, and he'll be the first to admit that the best of the best goes to the farmers markets. Eddie chuckles as he explains that on his farm, the women pick for the farmers markets, while the men pick for wholesale. The stone fruit he brings to the farmers markets requires a gentler touch, because it's riper, more fragile, and higher in sugar content, and therefore bursting with flavor. Eddie is committed to excellence, and he is one of many examples of why you'll find the best of the best produce at a farmers market.

to meet the farmers who grew your food. While an increasing number of grocery stores are now sourcing locally grown produce, crediting farmers with signage and life-size photos, this experience can never quite compare to meeting the authentic farmer in person, shaking his dirt-stained hand, exchanging cash and a smile for the freshest foods of the season, and sharing an expression of gratitude for the fruits of his labor.

The farmers market is a forum for connections and conversation. Think back to

your last trip to the supermarket. How many conversations did you have? Maybe one with the cashier, maybe two or three as you pushed your cart up and down the endless aisles. Now imagine the experience of shopping at a farmers market. If nothing else, you're guaranteed to have at least brief conversations regarding the weight and price of what you're buying. Admiring and sampling produce is the perfect jumpstart for a conversation with more substance, prompted by questions like: "What's at its prime this week? How is this grown? What's new on the farm? How do you like to prepare this?" With a few visits stashed in your

Authors Brigitte and Amelia strolling at the San Rafael Civic Center Market.

Jim Eldon and his son Miles of Fidler's Green Farm in Capay Valley. (Photograph by Curtis Myers.)

tote bag, you may even start to ask questions like: "How did your son Miles' football game go? Did the goats have their kids last week? Did you take any trips during your off season?"

There's even something endearing about the grumpy farmer; the one with the sun-dried face and the dirt in his fingernails who is here to sell you the best damn apples known to man. As you ask for a sample and make conversation, he's thinking, "You know they're the best. Just buy 'em and move on for goodness sake." Doesn't he remind you of your grandpa in an ornery mood? And while it might not be the experience you had anticipated, it's certainly authentic. Rest assured that it's not just you; some of those farmers have won Mr. Grumpy awards from market management a few years running.

The interactions that take place at a farmer's stand are the precious moments that make farmers markets unique. Only here do the eaters have the opportunity to build genuine relationships with the people that grow their food. Knowing your farmer gives you a deepened appreciation for all the time and energy your food embodies, and paints a more complete picture of the trials and tribulations that go hand in hand with farming. It is this connection and understanding that reinvigorates our confidence and trust in our food system. It is this connection that an increasingly urban population craves.

FARMER, MEET YOUR EATER

In the local food movement, we tend to emphasize the benefits to the consumer when we talk about building a connection to the farmer and the land that grows your food.

Swanton Berry Farm from Davenport, California.

But let's not forget that it takes two to tango, and like any healthy relationship, the benefits flow both ways. Only at the farmers market does the farmer have the opportunity to meet the eaters who enjoy the bounty of his or her endless hours of cultivating the land. Within this system of direct marketing, their food does not disappear into some anonymous container where the great care with which the farmer grew it becomes irrelevant. Rather, their food goes directly into the eaters' baskets or tote bags, or is savored right there on the spot. Here, the farmer will enjoy the satisfaction of hearing an eater rave about how their family devoured the cherries they bought last week, or how they can't seem to get the goat cheese chèvre off their mind.

While the farmers market is a venue often flooded with gratitude, it's also brimming with suggestions and requests. For the farmer that is open to consumer input and is willing to be somewhat flexible and fluid in his or her business model, this is a unique opportunity. They can hear directly from a diverse community of customers, ranging from moms and dads looking for the freshest foods for their families to executive chefs seeking out the most unique and flavorful ingredients for their seasonal specials. Chefs are known to ask a farmer to grow a particular food they could not otherwise buy. What a great way to have a menu that is different from everyone else's. Farmers learn what their customers love, what the market is demanding, and what oddball variety eaters wish they could find. Having such direct access to their customers, as well as embracing their gratitude and their requests, is both a feel-good experience and a business opportunity for small family farmers.

I love bringing home fresh ingredients from the farmers market, partly because the taste is unparalleled but also because I feel connected to the people who grew them. When asked, "What's for dinner?" I can't help but give credit to the tireless farmers that cultivated our food. "We've got little gem lettuce from Jesse, heirloom tomatoes from Ed, goat cheese from Patty," and so on. The food somehow embodies their energy and the heart of the land where they grew my food. I also appreciate having a more intimate understanding of the challenges my farmers are facing. Knowing that the peppers will be late because of a recent cold spell or that perfectly delicious lettuce might look a little weather worn from a recent rain helps me feel like a more engaged and understanding eater. Food has never tasted so good.

Andrew Brait of Full Belly Farm, all smiles.

FOOD WITH A FACE

After twenty years of running farmers markets, food in the supermarket feels lonely to me. The experience of pushing a giant cart past uniform pastel produce and processed foods in flashy packaging feels bland and disappointing. It fails to engage my senses. Not only can I not smell the produce but there's no one behind the display to answer my questions of how it's grown, how to prepare it, and what I should look forward to next week.

MEET A MARIN LEGEND
KEVIN LUNNY OF DRAKES BAY FAMILY FARM

Kevin is a third-generation cattle rancher in Marin County who recently undertook the role of steward of Drakes Bay Estero, one of the most ideal and pristine bodies of water for growing shellfish in California. The Estero embodies 85 percent of Marin County's shellfish-growing waters and 50 percent of California's. When asked what he loves about farming, he replies "Everything," and then goes on to explain with almost overwhelming passion and fervor that he has always enjoyed working with the animals, but now he has a very different answer than he did a few years ago. He loves the connection that he has with his consumers. "It's refreshing," he says, "and it reinvigorates your sense of purpose."

HOW TO SAVE THE WORLD
ONE RECIPE AT A TIME

BUY LOCALLY AND SEASONALLY

There is good reason why local food is the craze these days, why people are craving a deeper connection to their food—whole nutrient-rich food, food with a face, not to mention food that is incomparable when it comes to freshness and flavor. Slowly but surely, we are emerging from an era of American food culture where farmers went unseen and uncelebrated, where food may just as well have been grown in the supermarkets as far as the consumer was concerned, and where there simply

Top: The Marin/Sonoma County line.
Center: Dave Evans of Marin Sun Farms (r) and Doug Stonebreaker (l) of Prather Ranch Meat Co.
Bottom: Marin Sun Farms Butcher Shop.

Marin and Sonoma cows are truly happy cows.

weren't many alternatives to industrialized, highly processed food and, thus, not many opportunities to choose to eat something different. Eaters are seeking food with a sense of authenticity, and local farmers are stepping up to the plate.

The local food movement is blossoming around the country. In 2007, the movement made its official debut in *New Oxford American Dictionary* with the induction of *locavore*—someone who eats food grown within 100 miles of their home. There are plenty of communities on the forefront of the movement that would argue that it's beyond the budding stage; rather, that local food is booming. My community in Marin County, California, is one of them.

Due to phenomenal growing seasons, and decades of environmental stewardship dedicated to preserving farm land in Marin and neighboring counties, it's possible for even the amateur locavore to eat locally grown food 365 days a year. I'm inspired by the locavore who finds something to eat in the dead of winter in the Midwest. That takes ingenuity, an understanding of traditional ways of preserving food, and, of course, time. The hard realities of chilling winters in other parts of the country invigorate my commitment to eating locally, taking advantage of this one delicious opportunity— because I can.

This can be as simple as connecting point A, farm, to point B, table; the more direct the better. Compare the locally grown produce at your nearest farmers market to the shipments of fruits and vegetables that arrive at a produce terminal. While most farmers travel an average of one hundred miles or less to the farmers market, vegetable shipments travel on average sixteen hundred miles, while fruit shipments travel about twenty-four hundred miles before arriving at the produce terminal.[1] The closer you eat to the source of your food, the fresher, the more flavorful, and the more nutrient-dense your food will be. Shopping at farmers markets, participating in community supported agriculture (CSA), and planting fruits and vegetables in your own backyard are all exciting opportunities to taste what food aspires to be and to reestablish your sense of connection to where your food comes from.

While there are dozens of benefits to local food, freshness and flavor are the most attractive hooks that lure in eaters time and time again. While I'm amazed by the trials and tribulations that a tomato must endure to arrive in the United States in December; harvested before it's time, trucked thousands of miles, and sprayed with ethylene gas to create a perceived ripeness, I simply refuse to allow my palate to be wooed by a sense of pity. I'd rather wait patiently for a vine-ripened heirloom tomato,

25

Local means asparagus in the spring and grapes in the fall, otherwise you are looking at product grown south of the equator.

picked gingerly at its peak and offered to me the very next day by a farmer beaming with pride. It might as well be heaven on earth.

REDISCOVER THE SEASONS

One of the delicious consequences of eating local food is that the eater will be effortlessly reconnected to the seasons, countering one of the most remarkable "accomplishments" of the industrialized food system. Think back to your most recent trip to the supermarket. I wouldn't be surprised if you didn't blink an eye as you perused mounds of apples, oranges, blueberries, and peaches, or scanned rows of asparagus, tomatoes, sweet corn, and butternut squash. But Mother Nature would be shocked at the cross section of seasons represented on these shelves: a blend of spring, summer, fall, and winter from all corners of the earth. Again,

a remarkable "accomplishment" by inventive humans set on conquering anything that might be perceived as an inconvenience or limitation.

I believe that the imaginative people who dreamt of year-round abundance had good intentions. After all, what harm could be done by meeting the demand for blueberries in the middle of December? Little did they know that by surpassing the seasons, our sense of time would begin to blur, and we would lose our connection to the natural rhythms of the earth. We've grown accustomed to the luxury of satisfying our cravings regardless of the season. But for all that we've gained for the sake of convenience, we've made grave sacrifices in the realms of flavor, anticipation, and diversity, not to mention the health of our environment. Eating seasonally revives these elements and reconnects us to the cyclical nature of life.

MAKE CONSCIOUS CHOICES

It may sound rather prudish to resist produce that's not in season, to limit yourself to ingredients that come from local farmers or at least from the same hemisphere. To be a year-round locavore takes a tremendous level of commitment, and some devout locavores would argue for giving up particular exotic foods entirely. Tropical fruits, coffee, and chocolate all fall into this category of imports that I quite frankly am not planning on giving up anytime soon. I savor the occasional mango, pineapple, or banana. God forbid I give up chocolate. I think my body would go into shock.

I do, however, choose my imports wisely, fully aware of the consequences that come with them, and I would advise you to do the same. If I'm not eating locally grown, I'm looking for certified fair-trade and organic products, because regardless of where it's grown, my food dollars play a role in influencing how my food is grown and the conditions of the people who grow it. Yet, if the fruit or vegetable grows in my regional food shed, I will happily hold out until the food arrives in its native season, simply because I know it will be a more delicious experience well worth the wait.

SAVOR THE EXPERIENCE OF EATING
BE WOWED BY TASTE

Sadly, many eaters have forgotten the sensory experience of eating real food; food that drips with flavor, food that smells like soil and sunshine, food that catches your eye with vibrant color and an air of vitality. Once you've tasted fruits and vegetables at their prime you may never go back. It's not difficult to pass on a rock-like peach in the middle of December when you know that it will pale in comparison to the blushing peach that you savored last July. The farmers market is the perfect place for

eaters hungry to taste fruits and vegetables at their best.

I'd like to invite you to take the sensory challenge. First, visit the produce section at your local supermarket. Get really close to those tomatoes, melons, or grapefruits. Can you smell something . . . anything? Are the colors rich and vibrant, or do they look a little on the pastel side? Now take a stroll through your local farmers market and pay attention to your senses. With the abundance of sweet and savory smells, rich colors, and produce that feels ripe to the touch, I wouldn't be surprised if you experience something of a sensory overload.

BITE INTO A "BEND OVER" PEACH
ROSE AND MATTEO DESANTIS OF DESANTIS FARMS

During a summer market when peaches were at their height, I visited the stand of my friend Farmer Andrew Brait of Full Belly Farm. With endearing pride, he presented me with what he called a "bend over" peach. Curious, I asked what he meant by that. With a smile, Andrew explained that a "bend over" peach is a peach so ripe that the juice rains down the front of your face and your shirt if you don't bend over when you take a bite. A peach just isn't worth eating if it's not a "bend over" peach.

Learn to embrace it; this is nature's bounty at its best. Go ahead, taste, smell, see, and touch a revelation.

The convenience of shipping produce in from the southern hemisphere has robbed eaters of the excitement of embracing the changing seasons, not to mention undermined our food security and inflated our ecological footprints. Anticipating, savoring, and then bidding farewell to a season and its bounty is a grounding experience. When it comes to seasonal food, I suggest you learn to crave and celebrate what is abundant and then get creative in eating what's fresh and local in every way you can imagine. That way you won't miss it so much when it's gone, because you'll have had your fill of it during its season and also because you'll be too consumed with your newest love of the current season.

While the saying "Absence makes the heart grow fonder" may have been intended for loved ones, I'd argue that it also applies to food. If Jill's sweet summer corn from G & S

Jill Machado from G&S Farms, better known as "the corn lady."

29

Farms were always at my fingertips, I would miss the thrill of shucking my first ear of corn come June. Even the lines at the farmers market are an experience, rubbing elbows with other expectant eaters, all anxiously awaiting their first taste of summer. Having waited patiently for months, the first bite is always pure bliss.

"An apple a day keeps the doctor away" is a timeless plug for fresh fruit, but let's be honest. A fig, huckleberry, kumquat, pomegranate, persimmon, tangelo, or quince would fit the bill just as well. Eating what's in season encourages eaters to explore beyond the typical seasonless supermarket list: apples, oranges, bananas, baby carrots, and a bag of triple-washed iceberg lettuce. When presented with such a mundane experience of fruits and vegetables, I can understand why bored eaters fill their pantries with a cornucopia of flashy processed foods. Let go of some of your current staples and see how seasonal eating will naturally infuse your diet with variety—lots of nutrient-dense foods at their prime, just as Mother Nature intended.

CELEBRATE WHAT IS UNIQUE TO YOUR FOOD SHED

It's surprising to me that a country so proud of its diversity and the freedom of its citizens to express their unique individuality has adopted such a monotonous food culture. Have you ever noticed that the menu at a fast food or chain restaurant is the same regardless of where you are in the U.S.? Whatever happened to tasting the uniqueness of region? San Francisco Sourdough, New Orleans Creole, and New England Clam Chowder used to be a part of the

EAT SLOW FOOD

In 1986, upon the opening of a McDonald's in Rome's Piazza Spagna, Carlo Petrini and a group of gastronomically oriented friends planted the seeds of a delicious protest, marking the unofficial beginnings of the slow food movement. Petrini and Slow Food's, now eighty thousand members in 850 chapters worldwide, believe that everyone has the fundamental right to pleasure and consequently the responsibility to protect the heritage of food, tradition, and culture that make this pleasure possible. The movement promotes good, clean, and fair food, believing that "the food we eat should taste good; that it should be produced in a clean way that does not harm the environment, animal welfare or our health; and that food producers should receive fair compensation for their work."[2]

experience of visiting a region. The same can be said for fruits and vegetables. The monocultures that define industrialized agriculture are steadily replacing our most long-standing regional food traditions. Not only do they compromise the diversity and therefore the security of our food production, monocultures also make for terribly boring eating experiences. At the farmers market, you'll find unique heirloom varieties of fruits and vegetables that are specific to your region, cultivated from seeds saved by generations of farmers. The diversity that you'll encounter will not only wow your taste buds but will help you rest assured that our food security is in good hands.

VOTE WITH YOUR FORK
KEEP LOCAL LAND IN AGRICULTURE

Supporting local farmers directly helps them run viable businesses and ensures that local land will continue to produce food rather than succumb to development. The rate at which we've lost farmers since 1915 is astounding. At that time, more than 30 percent of the U.S. workforce was engaged in farming and 50 percent of the U.S. population lived in rural areas. Today, less than 2 percent of Americans farm for a living, and a mere 10 percent live in rural areas.[3] The Green Revolution, with all its fancy inputs and machinery, enabled larger farms to become more "efficient" and more "productive" than smaller family-run

operations, putting many of them out of business. The consolidation of family farms is overwhelming; between 1950 and 1997 the number of farms in the U.S. dropped from 5.4 million to 1.9 million,[4] with the average farm size more than doubling, increasing from 216 acres in 1950 to 487 acres in 1997.[5]

Despite these discouraging numbers, there are handfuls of small family farms scattered across the country hanging on to the traditions

Albert Straus, owner of the first organic dairy west of the Mississippi—a multi-generational farm reinventing itself.

MEET A FIRST GENERATION FARMER

David Retsky grew up in Beverly Hills, not having a clue where his food came from. He is the son of a doctor and claims no genetic predisposition to farming, as no one else in his family has a green thumb. In his early twenties, looking for his sense of purpose and a connection to the earth, he worked on farms in England, Israel, New Zealand, and Hawaii, volunteered for a year at the Fairview Gardens in Santa Barbara, and studied Agroecology at UC Santa Cruz. In 1999, he placed an ad in a handful of newspapers: "Organic farmer looking to lease 6–12 acres. Must have water." Today, his farm, County Line Harvest, is thriving, selling at local farmers markets and wholesale to a handful of Bay Area restaurants. David and his crew grow a variety of leafy greens and vegetables on thirty-two acres in Marin County. (Photograph by Curtis Myers.)

of generations past. They are the brain trusts of future local food systems, and their viability is in the hands of local eaters—in the form of your food dollars. Direct marketing opportunities and the exploration of niche markets are pivotal in creating successful self-sustaining farms that can provide living wages for the families and the workers that cultivate the land.

The viability of the small-scale family farm is also essential to ensuring that future generations have an interest in farming. The average age of U.S. farmers is quickly approaching sixty, with only 5.8 percent of our three million farmers under the age of thirty-five. With over three hundred million Americans to feed, we are in desperate need of the next generation of farmers.[6] For nearly a century, the large majority of farm kids that would have become farmers have been pursuing more secure careers and adopting the comforts of urban living, largely because they watched their parents struggle to make ends meet.

Now with our current farmers on the edge of retirement, the need for young, bright, vivacious men and women, both multigenerational farm kids and energetic urbanites, is becoming more and more prevalent. Two absolutely essential elements in maintaining the feasibility of local food systems are ensuring that this next generation of farmers has access to productive land and

also that there will be thriving local markets where they can sell their farm-fresh goods direct to consumers. We must do the leg work now—protect land from development, establish local markets, and all the while, pass along the collective wisdom of today's farmers to the men and women who will soon be feeding us and the next generations.

INVEST YOUR DOLLARS IN A HEALTHY FOOD SYSTEM

I'd like to suggest that we are doing ourselves a great disservice by skimping on our food budget. Even with rising food prices making front page news around the world, Americans still spend the lowest average percentage of their disposable income on food—just under 10 percent. Compare that to 14 percent in France, 22 percent in Mexico, 40 percent in India, and 50 percent in Indonesia. This is possible in large part because of the U.S. Farm Bill and its generous subsidies for the production of corn, soybean, wheat, rice, and cotton. These commodity crops are at the root of nearly all processed foods, which explains why a dollar will buy you more calories in the middle rows of the supermarket where the foodlike substances reside than in the produce section, and why a McDonald's cheeseburger can slide in just under a buck. Americans have come to expect and demand outrageously low food prices.

Patty Karlin of Bodega Artisan Cheese from Sonoma County.

However, there are hidden costs to our cheap food. These include costs to our health, with obesity and diabetes reaching epidemic levels; costs to the environment, with monocultures and confined animal feed operations depleting our soil and flooding waterways with chemical fertilizers, pesticides, and animal waste; and costs to the viability of food systems worldwide, with our subsidies undermining the production of these grains in other countries, making it so these farmers simply can't compete in a global market.

A young mother was at the market one day with her three young children. She was telling me that she had recently budgeted an extra $500 a month for food. Shocked, I asked why. She explained that her health insurance had just been raised $600 a month, and not able to afford it, she signed up for the larger deductible insurance plan and added the money she saved to her food budget. She explained, "My thought is that we will eat better and get sick less."

By investing a little more in our food, sourcing fresh fruits and vegetables directly from local farmers, and taking the time to cook our own meals, you and your family will be saving the world one recipe at a time. Local family farms will stay in production and continue to be responsible stewards of the land. Witnessing how Americans are investing their food dollars, the U.S. government will be pushed to reevaluate the Farm Bill, a policy that not only affects Americans but also farmers and eaters around the world. Perhaps we'll even solve the health-care crisis. Consider it preventative health insurance.

There is no doubt that there will continue to be a demand for food, and it is the food we eat today that will dictate the nature of our food systems tomorrow. At every meal we essentially cast a ballot for the future of food. Our votes—our food dollars—will be pivotal in ensuring that fresh, flavorful, nutrient-dense

Prather Ranch Meat Co.

food is available for our children and our children's children.

TAKE A STEP TOWARD SHRINKING YOUR ECOLOGICAL FOOTPRINT

I believe that we should be able to grow our own food, at least the large majority of it. Eating locally grown seasonal foods, direct from small family farms, ensures that local land stays in agricultural production. The more we import foods from overseas, the more we depend on global markets for our food and thereby put ourselves at the mercy of foreign producers. Only in the last fifty years have we shipped produce so freely around the globe. That's a very short time in context of humankind's ten thousand years of agrarian history.

And while America has been able to take advantage of inexpensive food produced in developing countries in addition to our own oil intensive subsidized crops, the days of cheap

fuel are dwindling. In the very near future, imported or subsidized food may actually reflect the true cost of its production and transport. In the mean time, it is imperative that we support our local growers. Paving over their rich soil to make way for cookie-cutter track houses and shopping plazas only compromises our food security. By investing our dollars directly in our local farmers, we are investing in the future viability of our food shed.

There's a lot of talk about our ecological/ carbon footprints these days. Quite frankly, I didn't quite know what that meant until recently. As with most new modes of thought, the terms used to describe ecological footprints are an acquired vocabulary: biological capacity, ecological reserve, ecological deficit, overshoot, and global hectares are all new to me. I still don't totally grasp it, but here's my best shot. Essentially, our footprint takes into account the resources required for us to maintain our lifestyle. There are many choices that factor into our ecological footprint, including the size of our home, how much water we consume, how often we use our heat or air conditioner, the car we drive, the distance we commute, whether or not we use public transportation, how many "toys" we own, how often we travel, and, of course, the food we eat.

As many people are becoming more conscious of the consequences of their consumption habits, it's easy and understandable to feel overwhelmed by the tough realities of our collective footprints. The Global Footprint Network estimates that today humanity's Ecological Footprint is over 23 percent larger than what the planet can regenerate. In other words, it now takes more than one year and two months for the earth to regenerate what we use in a single year.[7] With consumption habits on the rise and developing countries aspiring for an American standard of living, it's certain that this number is increasing.

The food production system accounts for 17 percent of all fossil fuel use in the U.S.[8] In the typical feedlot system, an average of 35 kcal of fossil energy is used to produce 1 kcal of beef protein.[9] Processed foods require even more energy inputs: over 500 kcal/kg for canned fruits and vegetables, nearly 2,000 kcal/kg for frozen fruits and vegetables, and approximately 15,500 kcal/kg for breakfast cereals.[10] Eating fresh, locally grown food and choosing smaller portions of organic and humanely raised

meats are steps we can all take to lessen our impact on the planet. We can save a significant amount of fossil fuel by eating regional foods, and farmers can help by minimizing inputs, as traditional fertilizers and pesticides contain petroleum themselves, and by using more people power to manage weeds and harvest crops, thus lessening their dependence on fuel-consuming machinery.

In Barbara Kingsolver's *Animal, Vegetable, Miracle*, Steven L. Hopp proposes that "if every U.S. citizen ate just one meal a week (any meal) composed of locally and organically raised meats and produce, we would reduce our country's oil consumption by over 1.1 million barrels of oil *every week*.[11] While it's easy to feel overwhelmed by the feeling that we're not doing enough to shrink our ecological footprints, eating locally grown food may very well be one of the most tangible and delicious choices we can make in our efforts to tread more lightly on the earth.

A SIMPLE LIST OF SIGNIFICANT THINGS WE CAN ALL DO TO SAVE THE WORLD

Of the following challenges presented, I encourage you to take only one of them at a time until it becomes a habit. The immense task of "saving the world" can be overwhelming, but together, making small but significant changes to our daily actions, we can create change locally. Communities creating change locally can affect change regionally; regional communities can create change nationally; and nations can produce change internationally. The repercussions are endless, and they start with you today.

- Support local agriculture by shopping at the farmers market.
- Embrace what's in season.
- Choose organic when available. When it's not available, start a conversation to learn why.
- Choose quality over quantity when you eat meat, poultry, dairy, eggs, or fish.
- Choose fair trade when purchasing imported goods like coffee, chocolate, and tropical fruits.
- Grow your own food. Join a community garden. Plant a fruit tree.
- Bring your own reusable tote bags and produce bags to the farmers market and grocery store. Play a game with yourself— how few single-use bags can you use?
- Shop for bulk goods at your local market. Bring your own jars to reduce packaging.
- Enjoy leftovers. Get creative so that food doesn't go to waste.
- Compost at home. It's a fun, eco-friendly way to shrink the waste you would normally send to the landfill.
- Recycle. Reduce. Rot. Reuse and reuse and reuse.
- Replace burned-out light bulbs with energy-saving compact florescent lights. Turn the lights off when you leave a room.
- Turn off the faucet when you're not using the water. It's a precious resource!
- Take public transportation, walk, bike, and carpool. Group your errands.
- Frequent locally owned businesses that share your values.
- Ask your favorite restaurant if they've ever considered using local seasonal ingredients.
- Introduce yourself to your neighbors. Build a community.
- Get informed. Learn the truths about the industrialized food system and a more sustainable food system. To get started, see Industrialized Conventional vs. Local Sustainable Agriculture on page 190.
- Invest your dollars wisely. The food, the services, and the consumer goods you buy are all a reflection of your values.

You vote for the world you want to create with every dollar you spend.

IT'S TIME TO LEAVE FAST FOOD AND GO BACK TO SLOW FOOD

RIPPLE EFFECTS OF OUR FOOD

There is something meditative about throwing a pebble to the middle of a pond and watching the ripples follow one another to shore. Moments like these used to make me contemplative—now they just remind me of food. The ripples are a simple metaphor that remind me that my decisions, including the food I choose to eat, have consequences that extend far beyond my self, touching many other people and ultimately shaping the world we live in.

That may be a lot of pressure to put on a meal, but the way that we invest our food dollars has a significant impact on our food systems. Every time we eat, we have an opportunity to vote for the type of food system we'd like to see. For most people, that's three votes a day. At a time when it's easy to feel overwhelmed and helpless by all the gloom and doom in the news about climate change, global food shortages, peak oil, water wars, and the like, voting with your fork suddenly becomes a source of empowerment to create positive change. And it's not just the environment that will benefit from your locally grown meal— your health, your family, and your community will also feel the ripples.

RIPPLE ONE: YOU

I am not a nutritionist. I cannot give you a nutrient-by-nutrient breakdown of a perfectly tart cherry or a vibrant bunch of deep green kale. I can, however, like you or like any eater following his or her instincts, decipher what real food is. By real food, I mean fresh whole foods that haven't lost their flavor or nutritional value due to lengthy commutes—foods that help you slow down the dizzying pace at which we live our lives and foods that both fill our belly and nourish our soul.

Yet judging from the rotating fad diets, the ever-changing food pyramids, the endless discovery of miracle foods and their demonized counterparts, American eaters are confused and are finding themselves in the depths of an eating disorder. We've lost our food culture, allowing instincts and traditions that would help us decide what to eat to be overpowered by percentages on nutritional fact boxes and multi-million-dollar marketing campaigns. The resulting statistics are staggering: "Nearly 119 million American adults, 65 percent of the population, are currently overweight or obese."[1] It has been projected that one in three Americans born in 2000 will develop diabetes during their lifetime.[2] "The direct and indirect costs of obesity in America are more than $117 billion annually."[3] For the first time in two centuries, American children have a shorter life expectancy than their parents.[4]

Returning to whole, fresh, nutrient-dense foods is as close to a silver bullet as you can get when it comes to repairing the tattered

David Little's dry farmed potatoes. (Photograph by Steve Quirt.)

food culture we have created. Sourcing fresh ingredients from local farmers, ranchers, bakers, cheese makers, and so on, effortlessly rids our diet of additives, preservatives, and partially hydrogenated oils. Because the foods of these artisans are intended to be enjoyed within a day or two, if not hours, of when they were harvested or prepared, the extra ingredients—you know the ones that you have to sound out phonetically—aren't necessary.

What fresh fruits and vegetables from the farmers market lack in additives, they make up for in nutrients. The density of nutrients in fruits and vegetables begins to decrease the moment they are harvested, a natural occurrence after being picked from the lifelines of sun, soil, and water that sustained them.

Thanks to refrigeration, we've been able to keep foods from spoiling as quickly as they would otherwise. But the convenience of storing food for weeks at a time is both a blessing and a curse; it has freed us from the inconvenience of picking up food daily and simultaneously robbed us of the experience of eating fresh nutrient-dense food. Take bagged spinach for example. According to researchers at Penn State, spinach stored at 39 degrees F lost nearly half its nutrients in eight days. When stored at 68 degrees, the same amount of nutrient loss occurred in only four days. The average temperature maintained by household refrigerators is 40 degrees F.[5] North Carolina State found that ideal shipping conditions for leafy greens entail cooled containers with high humidity and temperatures of 34 to 38 degrees F. A head of lettuce can be "held" for 2 to 3 weeks at 32 degrees F and 95 percent relative humidity.[6] That's a lot of embodied energy for a food that has lost much of its nutritional value in transport. Even within our ingenious global distribution maze, "fresh" produce that has traveled thousands of miles, braved the chill of refrigerated shipping containers, and changed hands a multitude of times cannot compare to fresh produce that has traveled on average 150 miles or less and is sold by the same hands that harvested it. Our bodies can surely feel the difference.

In addition to nourishing our bodies, real whole foods also have a knack for nourishing our souls. In a world where so much of our day is consumed with fast-paced, virtual, and oddly disconnected activities, whole foods offer the eater an opportunity to slow down. Inevitably, they take a little longer to prepare.

David Little harvesting his dry farmed potatoes. (Photograph by Steve Quirt.)

I have yet to see a single potato at our farmers market prepackaged in plastic and ready for the microwave—and hallelujah for that. David Little's potatoes require a bit more handling. A gentle scrub will wash the fresh dirt off and will also provide you an opportunity to do something with your hands, something physical, and something intrinsically human. Like skipping rocks at a pond, preparing food can be a grounding experience if you can make the time to embrace it. It can be Zen.

RIPPLE TWO: YOUR FAMILY

Some of my best parenting moments have happened in my kitchen. While I would prepare dinner, my children would take turns sharing whatever was on their mind as they sat on wooden stools—elbows on the countertop, chin in their hands. This was my time to impart values—to reflect on the happenings of their days, to evaluate what went wrong or right, and to talk about how we could learn from their experiences. I cherish those evenings cutting fresh French fries, making stew, stirring the béarnaise sauce, and simultaneously raising my three children.

Eating meals together is the ideal way to build a family. Unfortunately, dinnertime is a time that many households are missing out on. We've created a multitude of reasons not to share meals together—parents are working late, the kids are at practice, we don't like to

eat the same foods, or our favorite TV show is on tonight. Of course, there are circumstances that make sitting down to a five-course feast on a weeknight feel close to impossible. I get that. At one time, I too was juggling multiple roles as mother-of-three, wife, daughter, friend, business-owner, volleyball coach, and amateur athlete. It was a lot to balance, and I'll admit that I welcomed the occasional convenience of fast food and prepackaged dinners. But despite the ease of that lifestyle, we would always gravitate back to sharing a home-cooked meal at the table. More often than not, the meal helped to put everything into perspective and allowed us to take a breath in our busy lives.

Imagine a meal without "to go" boxes, without children text messaging (omg!), without the distraction of a TV. I have vivid memories of a KFC commercial that went something like this: Dad pulls into the driveway. Mom calls the kids to dinner from their separate rooms. Kids put down their video games and pull themselves away from their engrossing MySpace page. Plates and forks are gathered. Plastic bags are set on the table from which the family pulls boxes of fried chicken, mashed potatoes, coleslaw, and biscuits. "Isn't it time that we shared a meal together?" the wise narrator poses. Is this really what we've come to? The French in me is disgusted (how typical), and the American in me is embarrassed. This odd rendition of a family meal, and the fact that many eaters don't even blink an eye, suggests that we've given up on the possibility of enjoying the full experience of sharing a meal together—from gathering fresh ingredients, to preparing the meal, to setting the table, to breaking bread, to simply enjoying one another's company.

Now imagine a meal where your family joined you in seeking out the freshest ingredients of the season, in preparing the meal, and in being present at the table. A trip to the farmers market will heighten your child's understanding of food and where it comes from—specifically that it does not grow in supermarkets. I've found that kids are more willing to try new foods when they have the opportunity to explore them firsthand in a vibrant and engaging environment. And without the flashy marketing schemes and cartoon sales reps that attract kids to foodlike substances like Fruit by the Foot, Cheetos, and Cocoa Puffs, you can be sure that something else might catch their curiosity, like Clarence's gemlike pomegranates, Jim's purple carrots, or Rosa and Mateo's Buddha's hand.

When you take those ingredients home, give your kids a role in the kitchen. Yes, preparing a meal takes time, or at least easy slicing and dicing does, but many hands make light work. It's time that our children were as skilled with a paring knife as with their PlayStation controller. Consider your family a team of chefs, except

that you get to enjoy the delicious results of your efforts. Children who participate in the prepping and cooking of a meal are more likely to eat that meal with gratitude and a sense of pride in their contribution.

When the meal is ready to enjoy, sit down together, get rid of the distractions, and establish traditions. Give your family the gift of being present with one another. It takes practice to slow down, especially given the pace at which we operate, but both the physical and spiritual health of your family depend on it. By sharing a meal with your family, especially one made from fresh local ingredients, you are passing along a food culture with a conscience, creating future eaters that will take the time to nourish themselves with real food—ensuring the health of future generations. By breaking bread together, you're also breaking boundaries and building relationships, strengthening the bonds that tie your family together and that will support you throughout the years, allowing the ripples to grow wider.

RIPPLE THREE: YOUR COMMUNITY
Extending beyond your personal health, beyond the health and connectedness of your family, your food choices also have tangible impacts on the health and vibrancy of your local community. Eating locally grown produce, slicing locally baked bread, drinking local milk, and savoring meats from your local rancher not

only tastes better but also ensures the viability of your local food system. Keeping these people in business may be one of the most important things we do in terms of maintaining our food security, because at the end of the day we need to have the capacity to feed ourselves.

Choosing locally grown food simultaneously supports the livelihood of local producers, fulfills our hunger for fresh quality food, and rebuilds the sense of connectedness to our community, which we have sacrificed by allowing ourselves to be swept away by the convenience of big industrialized agriculture. It is nearly impossible to feel connected to the extended community of people that have collaborated to bring you your food while shopping at the nearest chain grocery or buy-in-bulk superstore—even with the friendly greeter that meets you at the door. They're too big, too corporate, and the pockets of the shareholders are too deep and mysterious. There are great benefits to knowing where your dollar goes; it illuminates the consequences of your purchase and confirms your commitment to investing your money in products that embody your values. You can see the trickle down of your investment as it goes into the pocket of a farmer or the cash box of a mom-and-pop restaurant. These elements of traceability and transparency are precursors to trust and the foundation of a relationship that is mutually enriching. When it comes to human connections, building rapport

with local farmers, food purveyors, restaurants, and businesses fulfills our desire to be part of a community, to be able to go where everybody knows our name—think *Cheers*. Of course these relationships will take time, as most good things do.

In 2007, I had the opportunity to hear Judy Wicks, owner of White Dog Café in Philadelphia and founder of BALLE (Business Alliance for Local Living Economies), describe a living economy as one that ensures that economic power resides locally, sustaining healthy community life and natural life as well as long-term economic viability. Local sustainable agriculture plays a pivotal role in creating local living economies by nourishing the people of the community. Shopping at the farmers market is one important step we can all take to enrich the viability of our local food system. The next step is to leverage our influence as a customer at local cafés, restaurants, schools, hospitals, and corporate cafeterias to expand the availability of locally procured food.

The food we consume outside of the home, at the places where we work, play, learn, and heal, is equally central to our health and the viability of our local food producers, but unfortunately the vast majority of it remains stuck in the grasp of industrialized food chains. The convenience of industrialized agriculture and its savvy distributors make it all too easy for businesses to order exactly what they need for a static seasonless menu. It's time we start voting with our forks both at home and in our communities. Creating a demand for local food throughout our community will further the ripples that extend from our food choices, creating an opportunity for farmers and local food purveyors to grow and diversify their business while simultaneously making locally grown, fresh, nutrient-dense food available to the community at large.

RIPPLE FOUR: OUR PLANET

Today we're facing plenty of worldwide challenges on many fronts, most of which boil down to environmental and social justice issues. It feels like every other article I read these days addresses climate change, peak oil, the global food crisis, urban sprawl, a declining economy, natural disasters, and the like. Look closely and you'll see that these issues are all intimately interrelated and that the gloom and doom of one is fuel to the fire of another. Their interconnected nature is illuminated when what was thought to have been a solution to one issue deeply complicates another. For example, we had high hopes of clearing the peak oil hurdle when biofuels arrived on the scene. Enamored with the idea of liberating ourselves from foreign oil, we overlooked the consequences of using arable land to grow fuel

instead of food. Now with international food prices on the rise, the two issues simultaneously come into the limelight and challenge us to think of a solution that stacks functions and addresses not one but multiple factors. The ability to think creatively about how we address these issues and the willingness to see the complexities of the whole will be pivotal to creating positive change.

Eating locally grown food is one of the most delicious steps we can take toward shrinking our ecological footprint. By minimizing our food's commute, we're cutting down on the fuel consumed to transport the food, as well as the packaging and potential refrigeration. Investing in your local growers keeps local land in agriculture and in the hands of small family farms that typically use more sustainable growing practices of growing than large monoculture factory farms. Also, small local farms are more open to your feedback, more sensitive to market demands, and thus more flexible to meet those demands by altering their growing practices. Many farmers markets have seen a significant number of farmers transitioning to organic practices, encouraged by the growing demand for a more transparent and natural food system, free from chemical inputs.

Local food systems are multifaceted solutions to our multitude of challenges, simultaneously addressing global food shortages, obesity and diabetes epidemics, urban sprawl, dwindling local economies, and, yes, even climate change. Biotech and the Green Revolution clearly didn't serve America well, and I hope that other countries can learn from our mistakes. While we enjoy an abundance of grain-fed meats and processed foods, we also experience more diet-related illnesses than any other food culture—and the people that adopt our food culture often demonstrate the same symptoms. Letting go of the glamour of the American Happy Meal and the industrialized food system shouldn't feel like a grave sacrifice, but rather an empowering choice for a more healthful future.

I believe that this is our great opportunity and that now is one of the most exciting times to be alive in human history. The data may seem daunting and leave you prone to pessimism, but you only have to take a look at the people behind the movement or experience the thriving alternative industries they are creating to be overcome with a buoying sense of hope.

At a time when it's easy to feel overwhelmed by the immense challenges that face us, it's important to have daily opportunities to create tangible change. Your choice to eat food that is good for you, good for the farmer, good for your community, good for the land, and ultimately good for the planet, is a decision that rewards both your senses and your sense of what's right. With each bite you're voting for the future you want to see, the future you want your children to taste, the "bend over" peach you want your grandchild to savor. After all, life is too short to go with the naysayers. The time is now and the energy is hopeful.

SOUPS

VEGETABLE SOUP

4 cups chopped vegetables, trimmed

½ cup plus 1 tablespoon butter, divided

1 cup chopped onion (one variety or mixed)

2 tablespoons flour (rice flour preferred)

4 cups vegetable liquid (as mentioned in first step)

1 cup fine noodles

1 teaspoon herbes de Provence

½ cup cream

1 free-range egg yolk, whipped

Salt and pepper

Boil chopped vegetables in 4 cups water for 20 minutes. Drain vegetables, reserving liquid; set both aside.

Melt ½ cup butter and sauté onion for 1 to 2 minutes. Add flour, stir, and slowly add a little vegetable liquid. Stir and slowly add the rest of the liquid. Crush noodles slightly and add to the soup. Add herbs and drained vegetables. Check seasonings and cook for 20 minutes. Drain the vegetables, noodles, and herbs and put in a blender until smooth. Return to stove, stir in cream, and then stir in egg yolk and 1 tablespoon butter. Cook on simmer for 5 minutes. Salt and pepper to taste.

Makes 6–8 servings

This is a soup my grandmere prepared with whatever vegetables she had around the house at the time. My favorite combination of vegetables in this soup is pumpkin along with potatoes, leeks, or any kind of squash.

ONION SOUP

2 pounds onion, peeled and
  sliced
1/4 cup butter, divided
1 cup flour
3 quarts hot beef broth
Salt and pepper
1/2 cup sherry
1 baguette French bread
  (preferably stale), cut into
  paper-thin slices
1 cup grated Gruyère cheese

Sauté onions in 3 tablespoons butter until soft and golden brown; add flour and broth little by little. Stir and cook gently for 25 to 30 minutes. Add salt, pepper, and sherry.

Meanwhile, butter individual fireproof soup bowls with remaining butter. Toast the bread slices in a toaster. Line bowls with the toasted bread. Add a layer of cheese, a ladle of the onion soup, (just enough to moisten the bread), and continue layering until the dish is full. Finish with a layer of cheese. Broil until well browned.

Makes 6–8 servings

RAW SWEET CORN & CASHEW CHOWDER

3$\frac{1}{4}$ cups fresh yellow corn, divided (from 4 large ears)

2 cups water

$\frac{1}{2}$ cup raw cashews

6 tablespoons extra virgin olive oil

1 small clove garlic

2 teaspoons kosher salt

1$\frac{1}{2}$ teaspoons chopped cilantro leaves

Freshly ground pepper

In a blender, combine 2$\frac{1}{4}$ cups corn with the water, cashews, olive oil, garlic, and salt; purée until smooth. Pour the soup into bowls. Garnish with remaining corn, cilantro, and a sprinkle of pepper.

Makes 4 servings

CREAM OF WATERCRESS SOUP

3 tablespoons butter

1 large bunch watercress leaves, rinsed and patted dry

1 red potato, peeled and thinly sliced

Salt and pepper

3 tablespoons flour

3 cups chicken stock

½ cup heavy cream

Watercress leaves for garnish

In a saucepan over medium-low heat, melt the butter. Add watercress, potato, salt, and pepper; cook for 15 minutes, covered with a buttered round of wax paper and the lid, stirring occasionally. Add the flour and cook, stirring, for 3 minutes. Add the stock; bring to a boil and then simmer, stirring occasionally, for 15 minutes more.

In a food processor, purée the soup in batches and return to pan. Add the cream and more salt and pepper to taste. Cook over medium-low heat, stirring, until heated through. Serve in bowls and garnish with watercress leaves.

Makes 4 servings

CREAM OF SPINACH & MUSHROOM SOUP

$^{1}/_{2}$ cup clarified butter

1 pound fresh mushrooms, sliced

2 tablespoons flour

1 quart organic milk

1 quart half-and-half

3 tablespoons chicken base

1–2 bunches fresh spinach, chopped and blanched

1 leek, thinly sliced

Nutmeg for garnish

Melt butter in a stockpot over medium heat and then sauté the mushrooms quickly. Whisk in enough flour to make a dry roux. Next, add the milk and half-and-half and mix well. Dissolve chicken base according to directions on package and add to soup.

Drain the spinach and then add with the leek to the soup. Bring to a boil and simmer for an hour or so. If it gets too thick, add more milk. If it's too thin, make and add more roux (made on the side without mushrooms). You can experiment with the amount of chicken base, but too much makes it salty. When serving the soup, top each bowl with freshly ground nutmeg.

Makes 6 servings

SQUASH SOUP

1/4 cup butter

I large onion, chopped

2 pounds zucchini or other
   squash

3 rounded tablespoons farina
   (couscous kind)

2 quarts hot chicken broth

I cup chopped sorrel

I teaspoon chopped fennel
   green

I teaspoon chopped tarragon

Salt and pepper

Pinch of nutmeg

I free-range egg yolk

1/2 cup cream

Melt the butter and sauté the onion without letting it brown. Add the zucchini and farina, and stir. Add the hot broth and cook for 20 to 25 minutes. Then add the sorrel and herbs; cook for another 5 minutes.

Put the mixture through a sieve or in a blender. Return it to the pot and bring to a boil. Add salt, pepper, and nutmeg to taste.

Mix the egg yolk with the cream and add it to the soup at the last minute before serving. Do not allow the soup to boil after adding the egg yolk and cream.

Makes 6–8 servings

LEEK SOUP

1/4 cup butter

6 medium-size leeks, finely
    chopped (trim the tops and
    bottom of the leeks and use
    the remaining green, yellow,
    and white parts)

1/4 cup finely chopped shallots

1/2 cup finely chopped celery

2 medium-size potatoes, peeled
    and sliced

1 1/2 cups water

1 1/2 cups chicken broth

1/2 teaspoon pepper

1 cup cream, or 1 1/2 cups
    half-and-half or milk

Chopped chives for garnish

Heat butter in a saucepan. Add the leeks, shallots, celery, and potatoes and cook over low heat for 5 minutes. Add water, broth, and pepper. Cover and simmer for 20 minutes. Put mixture through a blender; blend in cream, half-and-half, or milk. Chill for 1 hour. Serve garnished with chives.

Makes 4 servings

This recipe is compliments of Dennis and Sandy Dierks, who moved to Bolinas in 1968. At the time, Dennis was a commercial artist working in San Francisco. Soon after their arrival they looked out at the front yard and said "Hey let's try something." They didn't have farming experience, but they learned quickly. What started as a field of leeks, has diversified into a farm that grows 30 varieties of organic vegetables, including 10 varieties of lettuce. Sandy says, "We're learning new things all the time. That's the beauty of farming."

CHILLED AVOCADO SOUP
TOPPED WITH CRAB

3 medium scallions, white and
    tender green parts only
2 medium garlic cloves,
    unpeeled
1 jalapeño, seeded and
    quartered lengthwise
1 tablespoon vegetable oil
3 Hass avocados, halved and
    pitted
1/4 cup finely chopped cilantro
    leaves
3 tablespoons fresh lime juice,
    divided
Salt and freshly ground pepper
1 cup cold buttermilk
3/4 cup bottled clam juice
1/2 cup ice water
1/4 pound cooked crabmeat
4 teaspoons crème fraîche
40 fried tortilla strips
Finely chopped chives
    for garnish

Preheat a grill pan to moderately high heat.

In a small bowl, toss the scallions, garlic, and jalapeño with the vegetable oil. Grill mixture 5 to 6 minutes, or until charred all over, turning occasionally. Transfer to a work surface and let cool.

Finely chop the grilled scallions and jalapeño and transfer to a medium bowl. Peel the garlic cloves, mash them to a paste, and add them to the bowl. Scoop the avocado flesh into the bowl and coarsely mash with a fork. Fold in the cilantro and 2 tablespoons lime juice. Season with salt and pepper.

In a blender, purée avocado mixture (about 1 cup) with buttermilk, clam juice, ice water, and remaining lime juice. Pour the soup into 4 bowls and top with crabmeat. Garnish each bowl of soup with a 1/2 teaspoon swirl of crème fraîche, 10 tortilla strips, and a sprinkle of chives.

Makes 4 servings

MEATS

HAPPY COW MEATLOAF

½ cup organic milk

1 free-range egg, beaten

1½ teaspoons Worcestershire
    sauce

1 teaspoon salt

½ teaspoon dried mustard

Several grinds pepper

1½–2 pounds grass-fed ground
    beef

1½ cups soft breadcrumbs

1 cup sliced button mushrooms,
    plus 2 whole mushrooms

½ onion, chopped

2 cloves garlic, chopped

4 tablespoons ketchup

2 tablespoons molasses

2 strips local bacon, chopped
    into small pieces

Preheat oven to 350 degrees F.

Combine milk, egg, Worcestershire sauce, and seasonings.
Gently mix in ground beef and all other ingredients except whole
mushrooms and bacon. Shape meat mixture into a loaf in a glass
pan, top with the whole mushrooms and the bacon. Bake 1 hour
or more depending on preferred doneness.

Makes 6 servings

CERTIFIED-ORGANIC LUNNY RANCH

The Lunny Ranch, which raises the cattle for Drakes Bay Family Farms, is situated in the heart of the Point Reyes National Seashore. The Pacific Ocean borders one side of the ranch and Drakes Estero borders the opposite side. This moist, marine environment provides for excellent pasture productivity, giving their cattle plenty to eat. Most of the time that the Lunny family has been on this ranch was spent producing milk in their grade-A dairy. In the mid 1970s, the dairy cows were sold and all their focus turned to their beef cattle herd. Today, the Lunnys produce certified organic and certified grass-fed beef on their certified organic pastures. On the ranch, they've been perfecting the art of raising grass-fed cattle for years. Their work is driven by the convincing evidence that grass feeding results in a healthier, more sustainable, and better-tasting product.

PORK
TAMALES

PORK TAMALES

3 packages of 40 cornhusks

4 (6-pound) grass-fed pork
    shoulders

3 large white onions, halved

Salt

15 black peppercorns

½ cup vegetable oil

Mole Sauce (see next page)

Fresh masa (5-pound bag)
    (find at a local Latin store)

2 (4-ounce) cans organic
    tomato paste

¼ cup local olive oil

To make the tamales, soak cornhusks for 2 to 3 hours. Put the pork in a large pot and cover with water. Add onions, a touch of salt, and the peppercorns. Cook over medium-low heat for 2 hours. Save the water for the mole.

Remove all fat from the pork. Shred the pork with your hands and then put back into the pot. Add the vegetable oil and reheat over medium heat. Pour in all of the Mole Sauce when the vegetable oil is hot. Add water, if needed, so that there is enough liquid to cover the meat. Simmer for 10 minutes.

Mix the fresh masa with the tomato paste and olive oil. Get your hands in there and really massage the masa. Invite the kids to wash their hands and come help. Thinly spread the masa in the middle of the cornhusks, leaving room to fold. Add meat and fold bottom of cornhusk up. Then fold sides of cornhusk in. Place in a steamer for 45 minutes on high. Remove and eat or freeze. Save any leftover meat for tacos.

To reheat the frozen tamales, thaw, keep in a moist cloth, and then microwave for 1 minute.

When talking with friends, share your recipes. We don't do that enough these days. This tamale recipe is my friend Robert's famous recipe—at least among his clients. The secret is in the masa, or dough. We had so much fun learning how to make tamales the way his mother taught him. What a great way to share recipes and cultures among friends.

MOLE SAUCE

6 dried pasilla chiles (soak in
   pot with pork until ready
   to make the mole)
4 dried guajillo chiles (soak in
   pot with pork as well)
8 ancho chiles
1 tablespoon olive oil
8 cloves garlic, chopped
1 white onion, chopped
3 fresh tomatoes, quartered
10 ladles pork water
1/2 teaspoon black pepper

To make the sauce, when the pork is done, soak the chiles in the pork water until it's time to make the mole.

Add oil to a skillet and sauté garlic, onion, and tomatoes for about 10 minutes, or until onion starts to brown. Take 10 soup ladles of the cooking water from the pork, trying not to get the peppercorns in the water and put in a large bowl.

Remove the chiles from the pork water. Seed and rinse the chiles without touching your face or eyes. Blend the chiles in the blender and then put in the skillet. Add the 10 ladles of water and pepper to the skillet and bring just to a boil with the tomato mixture. Pour on top of tamales.

Makes 5 dozen tamales

BARBECUED SPARERIBS

2 (2.5-pound) sides lean grass-
   fed spareribs
2 onions, sliced

BARBECUE SAUCE

4 tablespoons brown sugar
4 tablespoons Worcestershire
   sauce
4 tablespoons apple cider
   vinegar
2 teaspoons dry mustard
2 teaspoons liquid smoke
2 cups ketchup

Preheat oven to 300 degrees F.

Place spareribs in a shallow baking pan and cover with onions. Brown in oven for 20 to 30 minutes, remove and brush with Barbecue Sauce. Continue baking for 1 to 1½ hours, or until meat is tender. While baking, turn the ribs once to brown both sides and continue brushing with the sauce. Before serving, drain excess fat.

To make the sauce, mix all ingredients together.

Makes 4–6 servings

GRILLED LIME MARINATED FLANK STEAK

WITH CHIPOTLE HONEY SAUCE

2½ pounds grass-fed flank
    steak

1 canned chipotle chile,
    chopped

2 cloves garlic, chopped

1 tablespoon chopped cilantro

Salt

¼ cup vegetable oil

10 tablespoons lime juice

Pepper

8 slices crusty French bread

CHIPOTLE HONEY SAUCE

3 chipotle chiles, puréed

¼ cup local honey

2 teaspoons peanut oil

2 tablespoons balsamic vinegar

2 tablespoons brown mustard

½ cup freshly squeezed lime
    juice (about 4 limes)

1 clove garlic

2 teaspoons ground cumin

3 teaspoons cilantro (optional)

Salt and pepper

Place the steak in a large dish or baking pan. Mix together the chile, garlic, cilantro, salt, oil, and lime juice in a bowl and pour over steak. Cover and marinate in the refrigerator for 4 to 6 hours, turning occasionally.

Remove the steak from the marinade and season with pepper and more salt. Grill over high heat for about 5 minutes on each side for medium rare, 7 minutes per side for medium, or the desired doneness. Remove the steak from the grill and let rest for about 4 minutes. With a sharp knife, thinly slice the steak across the grain, at a sharp angle.

Serve the steak on top of the French bread and accompany each serving with several tablespoons Chipotle Honey Sauce.

To make the sauce, combine the chiles, honey, oil, vinegar, mustard, lime juice, garlic, and cumin in a blender or food processor and purée until smooth. Stir in the cilantro and season with salt and pepper to taste.

Makes 8 servings

USING LOCAL HONEY TO FIGHT ALLERGIES
FARMER AND BEEKEEPER SHELLEY ARROWSMITH

Honey contains bits and pieces of pollen, and as an immune system booster, it is quite powerful. But perhaps the most interesting therapeutic use for honey is as a natural remedy for seasonal allergies. The tiny amounts of pollen found in locally grown raw honey works over time to desensitize the body to a particular allergen—not unlike the way traditional allergy shots work. The best form of honey to take is pure, raw honey that hasn't been heated or extensively filtered. If you'd like to try honey for your allergies, contact a local beekeeper in your area and explain to him that you're interested in raw honey for allergies. It

seems odd that straight exposure to pollen often triggers allergies but that exposure to pollen in the honey usually has the opposite effect. In honey the allergens are delivered in small, manageable doses and the effect over time is very much like that from undergoing a whole series of allergy immunology injections. The major difference though is that the honey is a lot easier to take and it is certainly a lot less expensive. I am always surprised that this powerful health benefit of local honey is not more widely understood, as it is simple, easy, and often surprisingly effective.

SLOPPY JOES

1 (14.5-ounce) can whole
   tomatoes in juice, drained
1 large onion, chopped
4 cloves garlic, finely chopped
2 tablespoons unsalted butter
1 medium carrot, peeled and
   finely chopped
1 rib celery, finely chopped
1 teaspoon salt, divided
1½ pounds grass-fed ground
   beef chuck
1 tablespoon chili powder
1 teaspoon ground cumin
¾ teaspoon pepper
½ cup dry red wine
2 tablespoons Worcestershire
   sauce
1½ tablespoons packed
   brown sugar
4 Kaiser rolls, split

Purée tomatoes in a blender. Place the onion, garlic, and butter in a 12-inch skillet over medium-high heat and cook 4 to 5 minutes, or until onion begins to brown, stirring occasionally. Add carrot, celery, and ½ teaspoon salt; cook 4 to 5 minutes, or until vegetables are softened, stirring occasionally.

Add beef to pan and brown for 5 to 6 minutes, stirring to break up lumps. Add chili powder, cumin, remaining salt, and pepper; cook 2 minutes, stirring. Add puréed tomatoes, wine, Worcestershire sauce, and brown sugar. Boil, stirring occasionally, until sauce has thickened, about 6 minutes. Season with salt and sandwich the meat inside the rolls.

Makes 6 servings

SPICY CHEDDAR BURGERS
WITH CHILE MAYONNAISE

1¼ pounds lean ground
    grass-fed beef
1 cup grated cheddar cheese
¼ cup chopped cilantro
2 teaspoons chili powder
¾ teaspoon salt
1 teaspoon pepper

CHILE MAYONNAISE

1 lime, juiced
1 (4-ounce) can diced green
    chiles
¼ cup mayonnaise
¼ cup chopped cilantro
¾ teaspoon salt
4 Kaiser rolls, toasted
Tomato and avocado slices

Heat a large cast-iron or heavy-bottomed skillet to medium-high for 5 minutes.

Combine the beef, cheese, cilantro, chili powder, salt, and pepper in a large bowl; shape mixture into four patties.

Place in a skillet and cook 5 minutes on each side for medium rare, or to desired doneness. Serve burgers on rolls with Chile Mayonnaise and slices of tomato and avocado.

To make the mayonnaise, purée together all of the ingredients in a food processor until smooth.

Makes 4 servings

BEEF
TACOS

1 small Spanish onion
1 large heirloom tomato
½ head romaine lettuce
1 pound grass-fed ground beef
2 tablespoons ground mild
    red chile
2 tablespoons ground hot red
    chile or 2½ tablespoons
    chili powder
½ teaspoon oregano,
    preferably Mexican
½ teaspoon ground cumin
1 clove garlic, minced
1 teaspoon salt
¼ cup oil
12 soft organic corn tortillas
¾ cup grated cheddar cheese
¾ cup grated Monterey Jack
    cheese
Red salsa

Preheat oven to 225 degrees F.

Chop the onion and tomato and shred the lettuce; set aside in individual bowls.

Brown the beef in a frying pan, breaking it up with a fork. Stir in the chiles, oregano, cumin, garlic, and salt. Cook until the flavors blend, about 5 minutes. Once the meat is cooked, leave on a low simmer. Pour the oil into a large iron skillet and heat to medium-high. Place a tortilla in the pan for just a couple seconds, flip, and fold in half. Then with tongs, pick up and shake off excess oil. Lay onto paper towels to absorb oil and cover with another paper towel. Continue process until done. Fill the taco shells with the meat mixture. Top with lettuce, onion, tomato, and cheese. Serve with salsa.

Makes 6 servings

OVEN-ROASTED PRIME RIB
WITH TWICE BAKED POTATOES

1 (5-pound) boneless grass-fed
    prime rib
Salt

TWICE-BAKED
POTATOES

6 large baking potatoes,
    scrubbed clean
1/4 cup plus 2 tablespoons
    organic milk
Salt
2 1/4 teaspoons local salted
    butter
1 3/4 cups plus 2 tablespoons
    grated cheddar cheese

Preheat oven to 500 degrees F.

Coat the outside of the prime rib with salt. Place in oven and cook for 20 minutes. Reduce heat to 275 degrees F and cook 2 hours more. Do not open the oven door! The prime rib will be a perfect medium rare (130 degrees). Slice and serve with the Twice-Baked Potatoes.

To make the potatoes, preheat oven to 350 degrees F.

Pierce potatoes with a fork once or twice. Bake for 1 hour, or until potatoes are soft yet firm. Let potatoes cool slightly. Cut baked potatoes in half and scoop out the insides, making sure to leave about a 1/4-inch shell. Mash the potato flesh with milk, salt, and butter. Stuff shells with mixture and sprinkle tops with grated cheddar cheese. Place potatoes on a baking sheet and bake at 350 degrees F for 15 minutes, or until cheese is melted and bubbly.

Makes 4–6 servings

THE WAY MOTHER NATURE INTENDED IT

Mike and Sally Gale are always welcoming on their beautiful ranch in Chileno Valley, California. Sally believes that "the reason grass-fed is best is because that is the way Mother Nature intended things to be. Cows are not adapted to eating grains, especially corn, and they need a lot of chemicals to keep them healthy when fed that kind of a diet. Corn became popular right after World War II because a surplus made it a cheap feed for cattle. With government subsidies, this trend has continued and clever marketing has created a demand for corn-fed beef. We believe, however, that grass-fed beef is not only better for the environment but that it tastes better. One of the things that we have done that is good for the land is, we have fenced our cattle out of our creeks and planted native trees there to provide habitat for wildlife and prevent soil loss. Chileno Creek flows through our property into Walker Creek, which flows into Tomales Bay, one of the most pristine bays on the West Coast. With our efforts, salmon will return to spawn in Chileno Creek, as Steelhead do now. Neo-Tropical Songbirds flourish in our streamside willows, when only five years ago our creeks were bare and devoid of vegetation. Our neighbors have recently fenced off their creeks, creating several miles of protected habitat on private land."

BEEF WITH MUSHROOMS & WINE

2 pounds beef, thinly sliced
    into strips
6 tablespoons butter, divided
1 tablespoon oil
Salt and pepper
1 cup dry white wine
6 cups sliced mushrooms of
    your choice—shiitake,
    button, chanterelle, oyster,
    portobello, morel, etc.
Chives or chopped greens of
    scallions
1 tablespoon chopped parsley

Remove all fat from beef. Heat 3 tablespoons butter with the oil; when hot, add beef and cook a few minutes on high heat. Add salt and pepper, and stir. Add wine and mushrooms, and then cook a few minutes more. Add chives or scallions.

Arrange on platter and melt remaining butter and pour over browned meat. Sprinkle with parsley and serve.

Makes 6 servings

When I was a little girl, I was at my Grandmere's house in Bretagne and woke up one morning to find a big fat white-and-black bunny rabbit hopping all over the lanai. I was so excited that she had bought me a pet. "Ahhhhh, non, Cherie! It's dinner," said my Grandmere. OH MY GOD! What was this? A cute bunny rabbit for dinner, or for that matter a cute chicken or cow, and I have to see it before we eat it? Horrors. I didn't understand that when I ate, something died. Well, I learned—we all do—but I stuck it way back in my subconscious. It was simply easier. Why?

Because as an American, I was never exposed to that part of the food chain. We bought our meat at the grocery store; we saw the butcher cut up the meat but never an animal. These days the large chain grocery stores have moved even carving into the back. All we see is the nice packages with no relation to the animal it once was. Why are we so afraid to discuss or see death? If we choose to eat meat, then we should support a high quality of life for the animal and a humane death, being thankful for what the animal has given us.

RABBIT A LA BRETONNE

1 onion, chopped

1 carrot, peeled and chopped

1 cup red wine

1–2 cloves garlic, minced

1/8 teaspoon ground cloves

Several sprigs fresh fennel

1 bay leaf

1 sprig thyme

1/4 cup chopped fresh parsley

RABBIT

2–3 pounds rabbit meat,
   chopped into small pieces

2–4 tablespoons oil

2–3 tablespoons flour

Salt and pepper

1/2 cup bouillon

1 tablespoon chopped fennel

3 tablespoons tomato purée

2 cloves garlic

1 tablespoon mustard

1/4 pound pork, made into
   lardons

2–3 cornichons, chopped

1 rabbit liver

Fresh parsley, chopped
   (optional)

Croutons, for garnish

To make the marinade, mix all of the ingredients together.

Add the rabbit meat to the marinade and marinate in the refrigerator for several hours or, preferably, overnight. Turn the rabbit occasionally. When ready to cook, remove the rabbit from the marinade and shake off excess moisture, but do not dry. Reserve the marinade.

Preheat oven to 300 degrees F.

Heat the oil in a skillet. Dip the meat in the flour to absorb any moisture, and brown the pieces on all sides. Place in a baking dish and add salt and pepper. Add the reserved marinade, bouillon, fennel, tomato purée, garlic, and mustard. Bake for 45 minutes in a covered baking dish. Near the end of cooking time, add the pork and cornichons.

Remove the membrane from the rabbit liver by scraping it with a spoon. Discard the membrane and chop the liver into small pieces. When the rabbit has finished cooking, remove to a heated platter and stir the chopped liver into the pan juices. Cook the liver, pour juices and liver over the rabbit, and sprinkle with parsley if desired. Garnish with croutons.

Makes 4 servings

TENDERLOIN STEAKS

WITH CRANBERRY-PORT SAUCE & GORGONZOLA CHEESE

4 tablespoons butter, divided

2 large cloves garlic, sliced

I large shallot, sliced

I¼ cups beef broth, divided

I cup ruby Port

¼ cup dried cranberries

4 (6-ounce) beef tenderloin steaks (each about I inch thick)

Salt and pepper

½ teaspoon minced fresh rosemary

½ cup crumbled Gorgonzola cheese

Melt 2 tablespoons butter in a saucepan over medium-high heat. Add the garlic and shallot and then 1 cup broth, Port, and cranberries. Boil until reduced to ½ cup, about 8 minutes; set aside.

Melt remaining butter in a large skillet over medium-high heat. Sprinkle steaks with salt and pepper. Add steaks to skillet. Cook to desired doneness, about 5 minutes per side for medium rare. Transfer steaks to a plate and cover loosely with foil. Add rosemary, reduced sauce, and remaining broth to skillet. Boil 1 minute, scraping up browned bits. Season with salt and pepper, and spoon sauce over steaks. Top each steak with crumbled Gorgonzola cheese.

Makes 4 servings

GRASS-FED BEEF STEW

3 pounds lean grass-fed stewing
    beef, cut into large cubes
2 tablespoons olive oil
1 large onion, chopped
1 carrot, sliced
Salt and pepper
2 cloves garlic, chopped
2 tablespoons flour
2 cups hot red wine, such as
    Madeira
3 cups hot beef stock
1 tablespoon tomato paste
Fresh thyme
1 bay leaf
1/4–1/2 pound bacon, cut into
    pieces
1 1/2 pounds small white onions,
    chopped
3/4–1 pound button mushrooms
3 tablespoons butter
Chopped parsley

Preheat oven to 325 degrees F.

Dry the beef on towels and then brown in oil. Brown large onion and carrot, and season with salt and pepper; add garlic. Arrange meats and vegetables in a casserole, sprinkle flour over top and toss to coat the meat. Let meat brown in the oven and then stir in hot wine and stock, enough to barely cover meat. Add tomato paste, herbs, and bacon to the casserole; bring to a simmer on the stove and then cover and set in lower third of oven; simmer for 2 to 2 1/2 hours.

Meanwhile, sauté onions and mushrooms in butter for 5 to 6 minutes and set aside. Add onions and mushrooms to the meat 10 minutes before serving. When serving, sprinkle with parsley.

Makes 8 servings

MARIN SUN FARMS

Marin Sun Farms raises cattle, pigs, chickens, lambs, and goats, providing their community with grass-fed and pasture-raised meats and eggs. David Evans and his sister Julie can be found at the farmers market every Sunday. The native pastures and rolling hills of West Marin are a perfect home for livestock. The mild climate and rich soils support a variety of native grasses upon which livestock feed as they develop into healthy mature beef. Grazing animals are critical to sustaining healthy and productive open spaces, as the grazing process itself contributes to the annual regeneration of many native grasses.

The cattle of Marin Sun Farms are raised on pasture their entire lives. In addition to eating grass and an organic mineral mix, the cattle are supplemented with hay and/or silage when the pasture nutrient density is low. The cattle are raised locally on ranches around Point Reyes

Station, Marin County, and on partner ranches within the Bay Area Food Shed in Sonoma, Mendocino, and Humboldt counties. Dave and Julie purchase cattle that are guaranteed to be free of synthetic hormones and antibiotics. The following breeds have frequented their pastures and the pastures of their partners: Angus, Hereford, Gelbvieh, Holstein, Short Horn, and Red Angus. One hundred percent grass-fed beef has a rich and robust flavor not found in conventional, confinement-raised, grain-fed beef. Studies have shown that the types of fats found in grass-fed meats are much healthier. Grass-fed beef contains fewer Omega-6 fatty acids, which are believed to be linked to many diseases of humanity like heart disease and contains more of the healthy Omega-3 fatty acids as well as beta-carotene and CLA, another "good" fat.

LEG OF LAMB
WITH POTATOES & ONION

I onion, peeled and chopped

I teaspoon dried bay leaf,
  crumbled

I teaspoon fresh thyme

Salt and pepper

½ cup butter, divided

4 pounds potatoes (my favorite
  are Yukon gold), divided,
  peeled, and thinly sliced

2 cloves garlic, peeled and cut
  into small slivers

I (3-pound) grass-fed leg of
  lamb, at room temperature

Preheat oven to 425 degrees F.

Mix the onion with the bay leaf and thyme. Season with salt and pepper.

Grease the bottom of a 9 x 13-inch casserole with 2 tablespoons butter and layer half the potatoes in it. Sprinkle with half of the onion mixture. Add the remaining potatoes in an even layer and sprinkle with the remaining onion mixture. Dot with ¼ cup butter, cut in pieces, and moisten with warm water; the water should just cover the potatoes.

Place in the oven and bake for 1 hour and 45 minutes to 2 hours, or until there is hardly any water left in the bottom of the dish. Mash the rest of the butter with salt and pepper to taste. With a small pointed knife, prick the meat here and there, sliding in a piece of garlic with the knife blade at each incision. Spread the seasoned butter over the meat. Place the meat on top of the potatoes and roast for 45 minutes, turning meat to brown evenly. Turn off the oven and leave the meat inside for 5 minutes. Remove, carve, and serve.

Makes 6–8 servings

BEEF & CORN KABOBS

1 (4-pound) boneless grass-fed
    chuck roast
1½ cups citrus juice of your
    choice
1½ cups dry red wine
1½ tablespoons minced onion
1½ teaspoons Worcestershire
    sauce
1½ teaspoons dried thyme
¾ teaspoon dry mustard
¼ cup sugar
¼ teaspoon pepper
2 cloves garlic, minced or
    pressed
¼ cup butter, melted
¼ cup vegetable oil
5 medium-size ears white or
    yellow corn, husked and cut
    into 2-inch lengths
3 medium-size red bell peppers,
    seeded and cut into 1½-
    inch squares
2 large mild red onions, cut
    into 1½-inch pieces
8–10 medium-size oranges, cut
    into 2-inch slices

Cut meat crosswise into about 1½-inch-thick strips and then cube. Place meat in a large bowl.

In another large bowl, stir together juice, wine, onion, Worcestershire sauce, thyme, dry mustard, sugar, pepper, and garlic. Pour marinade over meat; stir to coat. Cover and refrigerate for at least 6 hours, or overnight, stirring occasionally.

In a small bowl, stir together butter, oil, and ⅓ cup of the marinade drained from meat; set aside. Discard remaining marinade.

On long, sturdy metal skewers, thread meat alternately with corn, bell peppers, onions, and oranges. Brush all over with butter mixture. Lightly oil a barbecue grill over a solid bed of hot coals or gas grill. Cook, turning and basting frequently with butter mixture, until meat is done to your liking; cut to test (about 15 minutes for medium rare). Make sure to thoroughly cook after last basting of marinade mixture is brushed on the skewers before removing from the grill.

Makes 8–10 servings

BEEF WELLINGTON WITH NEW
POTATOES & RED WINE GRAVY

PANCAKES

3 free-range eggs
6 tablespoons plain flour
5 ounces organic milk
Sliver of butter

BEEF WELLINGTON

1 (1-pound) beef fillet, middle
  section
Freshly ground black pepper
1 packet ready-rolled puff
  pastry
4 slices prosciutto
3 ounces smooth pâté
1 free-range egg
1 free-range egg yolk

GRAVY

2¼ cups chicken stock

To make pancakes, place the eggs and flour into a bowl and whisk together. Gradually add milk, whisking constantly to create a smooth batter that coats the back of the spoon.

Place a frying pan over high heat. Add a sliver of butter and, once the butter has melted, a ladle of the batter, tilting the pan to thinly coat the base of the pan with the batter. When the underside is cooked and golden, turn the pancake over and cook the other side until golden.

Tip the pancake out onto a plate covered with wax paper. Repeat this process to create a layered stack of pancakes and paper.

To make the beef, season the beef fillet with black pepper and then place into a frying pan over high heat. Turn the fillet to ensure even cooking. Remove when browned on each side and leave to rest in a warm place.

Roll the puff pastry to ¼ inch thick. Take two pancakes and place down the center of the pastry.

Add the prosciutto, arranging evenly over the pancakes.

Spread the pâté over one side of the beef and then place the meat pâté side down, onto the prosciutto.

Beat the egg and egg yolk together in a bowl. Then brush the egg over the clear area of the pancake and pastry, and fold around to enclose the beef.

5 ounces red wine

Dash balsamic vinegar

3 tablespoons butter

Salt and pepper

1 pound 2 ounces baby new
   potatoes, boiled until tender

Place the beef Wellington seam side down onto a baking sheet and brush with the beaten egg. Place in the refrigerator to cool for 30 minutes.

Preheat oven to 400 degrees F.

Remove beef from refrigerator and brush with egg once more. Bake for 25 minutes, or until the pastry is golden brown; bake longer if you do not like your beef rare. Let rest on a serving plate for 10 minutes. Serve slices of the beef on plates with the gravy poured over top and cooked potatoes on the side.

To make the gravy, place the stock and wine in a saucepan and bring to a boil. Reduce the liquid by one-third and then add the vinegar and butter, whisking well to dissolve. Season the sauce to taste with salt and freshly ground black pepper.

Makes 4–6 servings

CRUNCHY RICE, BEAN, & HAM SALAD

3 cups cooked rice

1 (15-ounce) can kidney beans, drained

1½ cups chopped celery

½ green onion, chopped

½ green bell pepper, chopped

1 (2-ounce) jar sliced pimientos

1 roasted red bell pepper

4–8 ounces cooked ham, sliced into thin strips

SWEET-AND-SOUR DRESSING

⅓ cup cider vinegar

3 tablespoons sugar

¼ cup salad oil

2 tablespoons Dijon mustard

2 teaspoons garlic salt

1 teaspoon pepper

¼ teaspoon liquid hot pepper seasoning

Mix all the ingredients together, and then mix in the Sweet-and-Sour Dressing.

To make the dressing, combine all the ingredients in a small pan. Heat to a boil and then mix with salad ingredients.

Makes 6–8 servings

GANDULES RICE

4 medium-size free-range
    smoked pork chops, diced

2 tablespoons olive oil

2 tablespoons sofrito

1 (4-ounce) can tomato paste

2 (4-ounce) small packages
    Sazon*

½ tablespoon Goya Adobo
    all-purpose seasoning

3 cups Rice Perla (available at
    Latin American stores)

1 (16-ounce) can Gandules
    Pigeon Peas, with juice

4 cups hot water, or enough
    water so it is level with
    the rice

1 (5-ounce) jar Manzanilla
    olives, drained

8 cilantro leaves

*This is a type of seasoned
salt. Typical ingredients include,
cilantro, achiote, garlic, and salt.
Some brands contain MSG, so
check labels carefully if you
wish to avoid the additive.

In a large skillet, fry diced pork chops in oil. Add the sofrito and sauté for 1 to 2 minutes then add the tomato paste and sauté for 1 to 2 minutes more.

In a large cooking pot, place pork chop and tomato paste mixture with all other ingredients except cilantro and simmer for 15 to 20 minutes. Simmer very low, uncovered, for 10 minutes. Fold the cilantro into the rice. Cover and simmer for 35 minutes.

Makes 8 servings

CHICKEN & EGGS

CHEESE SOUFFLÉ

¼ pound butter, melted, plus
    more for buttering dish
16 slices white bread, cut into
    ½-inch cubes and crusts
    removed
1 pound cheese, grated
    (I prefer cheddar)
6 free-range eggs
3 cups organic milk
1 teaspoon salt
1 teaspoon dry mustard
¼ teaspoon Worcestershire
    sauce

Butter an 8-inch soufflé dish. Line bottom of soufflé dish with one-third of the bread cubes. Then layer half the cheese, another third of the bread cubes, the other half of the cheese, and then the final layer of the bread cubes.

Beat the eggs with the milk and add salt, dry mustard, and Worcestershire sauce. Slowly pour mixture over bread and cheese. Now pour the melted butter over top. Cover and refrigerate overnight. Remove soufflé from refrigerator 45 minutes before baking.

Preheat oven to 350 degrees F.

Put soufflé dish into a 9-inch round baking dish or a casserole and pour water into dish until halfway up the sides of the soufflé dish. Bake, uncovered, for 1 hour and 15 minutes.

Makes 4 servings

CHICKEN
FAJITAS

12 flour tortillas

1 (16-ounce) can refried beans

2 tablespoons vegetable oil

2 medium onions, cut into
   $\frac{1}{2}$-inch wedges

2 large jalapeño peppers, finely
   chopped

1 large green bell pepper, cut
   into $\frac{1}{2}$-inch-wide strips

1 large red bell pepper, cut into
   $\frac{1}{2}$-inch-wide strips

2 large cloves garlic, crushed

1$\frac{1}{4}$ teaspoons salt, divided

2 whole boneless skinless
   chicken breasts, cut into
   $\frac{1}{2}$-inch-wide strips

1 teaspoon chili powder

2 tablespoons chopped cilantro

$\frac{1}{2}$ cup grated Monterey Jack
   cheese

Salsa

Steam tortillas as package label directs. In a small saucepan, heat refried beans; keep warm.

In a large skillet, heat oil over high heat. Add onions, peppers, garlic, and $\frac{1}{2}$ teaspoon salt; sauté 3 minutes, or until vegetables are tender. Add chicken, chili powder, and remaining salt; sauté 5 minutes, or until chicken is tender. Return mixture to pan; heat through.

Place chicken and vegetable mixture in a bowl on a large warm serving platter; sprinkle with cilantro. Arrange tortillas around bowl. Spoon beans into small bowl and sprinkle with cheese. Spoon salsa into another small bowl and serve.

Makes 6 servings

CHILE CHEESE SQUARES

2 pounds grated cheese
 (I prefer sharp cheddar)
2 (4-ounce) cans chopped
 green chiles (not drained)
18 free-range eggs, beaten
Salt and pepper
Paprika

Preheat oven to 350 degrees F.

Line a large baking sheet with grated cheese. Top with green chiles. Pour eggs over the top. Sprinkle with salt, pepper, and paprika and bake for 45 minutes. Cut into squares and serve.

Makes 50 (2-inch) squares

CHICKEN CACCIATORE

12 boneless, skinless free-range
 chicken thighs
Salt and freshly ground pepper
1 tablespoon extra virgin
 olive oil
1 small onion, peeled and
 chopped
1 medium green bell pepper,
 seeded and diced
1 (26-ounce) jar marinara sauce
¼ cup red wine
1 pound wide noodles or
 bow-tie pasta
Freshly grated Parmesan
 cheese

Rinse chicken and pat dry; season both sides with salt and pepper. Heat oil in a large skillet. Add chicken and cook for 5 minutes on each side over medium heat. Remove from skillet. Add onion to skillet and cook for 5 minutes. Return chicken to skillet and top with bell pepper, marinara sauce, and wine. Cover and cook for 30 minutes over low heat. Serve over hot cooked pasta, prepared according to package directions, and sprinkle with Parmesan cheese.

Makes 6 servings

Chile Cheese Squares

FREE-RANGE FRIED CHICKEN
WITH CREAM GRAVY

Oil or vegetable shortening for
    shallow frying

I cup flour

2¼ teaspoons salt, divided

1½ teaspoons pepper

3½ pounds free-range chicken,
    cut up

½ cup organic milk

½ cup water

Fill a large frying pan about ⅓ full with oil or shortening, and place on stove over medium-high heat. The ideal temperature is about 375 degrees F. Combine flour, 2 teaspoons salt, and pepper. Rinse chicken, but do not dry. Dredge in seasoned flour. Let stand while oil heats. Just before frying, dredge chicken in flour again. Reserve 2 tablespoons of the seasoned flour.

Cook chicken until golden, turning once, about 15 minutes per batch. Drain on paper towels.

Pour off all but 2 tablespoons oil from frying pan. Stir in reserved flour over medium heat, scraping up browned bits. Cook until golden and bubbly. Combine milk, water, and remaining salt, and stir in gradually. Cook 2 to 3 minutes, or until thickened, stirring the entire time. Season to taste. Serve cream gravy with chicken.

Makes 3–4 servings

RANCH HOUSE ENCHILADA CASSEROLE

3 to 4 boneless, skinless free-
  range chicken breasts
1 package thick (home-style)
  flour tortillas, taco size
1 (8-ounce) can green enchilada
  sauce
1 (16-ounce) can yellow corn
1 (16-ounce) can black beans
1 (16-ounce) jar chunky salsa,
  medium or hot
2 cups grated Monterey Jack
  cheese
2 cups grated cheddar cheese

Preheat oven to 350 degree F.

Boil the chicken and shred. Slice the tortillas in wide strips like lasagna noodles. Using a 9 x 13-inch pan, spread a light layer of enchilada sauce, then layer with tortilla strips, shredded chicken, a small amount of corn, beans, salsa, and both cheeses. Repeat this once more, ending with a third layer of sauce, tortillas, salsa, and cheeses. Bake for 45 minutes, or until enchiladas are hot throughout and the cheese has melted. Let sit for 5 minutes before serving.

Makes 6–8 servings

CHICKEN WITH RATATOUILLE VINAIGRETTE

RATATOUILLE

1 pound eggplant, sliced

2 teaspoons olive oil

¾ pound onions, coarsely
  chopped

6 cloves garlic, minced

½ teaspoon dried red
  pepper flakes

Freshly ground black pepper

2 tablespoons water

1½ pounds plum tomatoes,
  diced

2 medium red bell peppers,
  diced into ¼-inch pieces

1 medium green bell pepper,
  diced into ¼-inch pieces

1 tablespoon tomato paste

½ teaspoon sugar

½ teaspoon chopped fresh
  rosemary

1 bay leaf

1 medium zucchini, halved
  lengthwise and sliced
  ¼ inch thick

2 tablespoons red wine vinegar

Cayenne pepper

To make the ratatouille, preheat oven to 400 degrees F.

Line a baking sheet with foil and then place sliced eggplant on top. Bake until tender but not mushy, about 30 minutes. Cut into ½-inch cubes. Drain eggplant cubes in a colander.

Heat oil in a large skillet over low heat. Add onions, garlic, and pepper flakes. Season with pepper. Add water, cover, and cook about 6 minutes, or until onions are tender, stirring occasionally. Stir in tomatoes, bell peppers, tomato paste, sugar, rosemary, and bay leaf; cook 10 minutes, stirring occasionally. Add zucchini and cook until mixture is thick and zucchini is tender, about 10 minutes, stirring occasionally.

Preheat oven to 350 degrees F.

Combine tomato mixture with eggplant in a shallow 2-quart baking dish. Stir in vinegar. Season with cayenne. Bake 20 minutes. This dish may be prepared one day ahead.

CHICKEN

1½ cups chicken broth

1 thin slice onion

1 leafy celery top

2 cloves garlic, pressed and
    divided

1 bay leaf

6 boneless, skinless free-range
    chicken breast halves

¼ cup red wine vinegar

¼ cup extra virgin olive oil

3 tablespoons chopped fresh
    basil, divided

1 tablespoon chopped fresh
    parsley

Salt and freshly ground pepper

Fresh basil leaves

To make the chicken, pour chicken broth into a heavy 9-inch skillet. Add onion, celery top, 1 clove garlic, and bay leaf, and bring to a gentle simmer. Add chicken, cover and simmer 8 minutes; do not boil. Remove from heat. Uncover and let chicken cool in broth; drain chicken. This may also be prepared one day ahead.

Whisk together vinegar, oil, 1 tablespoon basil, and remaining garlic in a small bowl. Season vinaigrette with pepper. Slice chicken into thin strips. Toss with half of the vinaigrette.

Stir remaining vinaigrette, remaining basil, and parsley into ratatouille. Season with salt and pepper. Spoon onto plate. Top with chicken. Garnish with basil leaves and serve.

Makes 6 servings

CHICKEN BASQUAISE

1 tablespoon olive oil

2 large onions, diced

1 large clove garlic, finely
   chopped

10 green chile peppers, peeled
   and diced

2 red, orange, or yellow bell
   peppers, peeled and diced

6 very ripe tomatoes, peeled
   and diced

1 teaspoon thyme

2 tablespoons parsley

Salt and pepper

6 free-range chicken breasts,
   with skins

Flour

Add oil to a large skillet and sauté onions, garlic, and peppers. Once the onion has softened, add the tomatoes, thyme, parsley, salt, and pepper. Cover and cook over low heat.

Coat the chicken breasts with flour and add to the mixture of tomatoes and peppers. Cook for 30 to 45 minutes, or until chicken is done.

Makes 5 servings

This is one of my favorite recipes from the south of France. My Tantine Charlotte, my dad's sister-in-law, lived in a small village in Morlaas next to Pau. She was an incredible chef, but she never wrote any recipes down. The last time I saw her was two years ago, and I will always regret not sitting her down and asking her how she cooked all her fantastic dishes. But not all is lost—I have this one recipe. Who's your favorite family chef? Sit them down and record your family recipes so you don't lose all your family secrets.

CHICKEN KIEV

6 boneless, skinless free-range
　　chicken breasts
Salt and pepper
4½ teaspoons dried onion
　　flakes
3 teaspoons finely chopped
　　fresh parsley
6 thin slices ham
6 slices Swiss cheese
2 free-range eggs, beaten
Italian seasoned breadcrumbs

Preheat oven to 450 degrees F.

Pound chicken breasts to ¼ inch thickness. Sprinkle with salt and pepper, onion flakes, and parsley. Place a slice of ham and a slice of cheese on each chicken breast and roll up, with chicken completely covering the ham and cheese. Then roll in the beaten eggs and breadcrumbs. Secure with toothpicks. Bake in a greased pan for 10 minutes and then reduce heat to 350 degrees F and bake for 15 minutes more. Serve immediately.

Makes 6 servings

CHICKEN WITH DATES & APRICOTS

2 cloves garlic, minced

¼ cup orange juice

½ teaspoon ground cumin

¼ teaspoon ground cinnamon

3 tablespoons extra virgin
    olive oil, divided

4 boneless, skinless free-range
    chicken breasts

1 large onion, finely chopped

¾ cup chicken broth

½ cup dried apricots

½ cup dried pitted dates,
    halved lengthwise

1 tablespoon finely chopped
    cilantro

1 tablespoon finely chopped
    mint

Preheat oven to 350 degrees F.

Mix garlic, orange juice, cumin, cinnamon, and 1 tablespoon oil in a small bowl. Pour mixture into an airtight container. Add chicken and shake to coat. Refrigerate 1 hour.

Heat remaining oil in large skillet over medium-high heat. Add onion and sauté until golden brown, about 5 minutes. Add contents of airtight container. Sauté until chicken is browned on both sides, about 5 minutes. Using a fork, transfer chicken into a roasting pan, 4-quarts or larger.

Add broth, apricots, and dates to skillet with onion mixture; stir. Pour into roasting pan. Cover pan and bake for 45 minutes, or until chicken is tender. Stir in cilantro and mint, leaving a few mint leaves for garnish, and serve.

Makes 3–4 servings

JAMBALAYA

1 large yellow onion, chopped

1 cup diced celery

3 tomatoes, diced

1 (16-ounce) can chicken broth

3 ounces tomato paste

1½ tablespoons Worcester-
shire sauce

1½ teaspoons Cajun seasoning

1 pound boneless, skinless free-
range chicken breast halves
or thighs, cut into chunks

2 sausage hot links, sliced

1½ cups rice

½ pound large raw shrimp,
peeled and deveined

¾ cup chopped red, yellow, and
green bell peppers

Combine the onion, celery, tomatoes (with juice), broth, tomato paste, Worcestershire sauce, and Cajun seasoning in a 4-quart or larger slow cooker. Stir in chicken, sausage, and rice.

Cook on low heat for 5 to 6 hours or on high heat 2½ to 3 hours, or until chicken is cooked through, rice is tender, and most of the liquid is absorbed.

Stir in shrimp and peppers. Cover and cook on high heat 10 to 15 minutes more, or until shrimp is cooked through. Dish onto plates or in bowls and serve.

Makes 8 servings

CHICKEN WITH CREAM & MUSHROOM SAUCE

6 free-range chicken breasts,
  with skin
Salt and pepper
4 tablespoons butter, divided
3 tablespoons vegetable oil,
  divided
1 thin slice bacon
1 pound button mushrooms
1/2 lemon
4 shallots
1 1/4 cups white wine
1 teaspoon flour
1 1/4 cups crème fraîche

Season the chicken breasts with salt and pepper. Heat 3 table-spoons butter with 2 tablespoons oil in a large frying pan. Add the pieces of chicken and brown on all sides over medium heat.

Meanwhile, cut the bacon into small pieces. Dice the mushrooms and sprinkle them with the lemon's juice. Peel and chop the shallots. Gently fry the bacon in a frying pan without any fat; drain and set aside.

Heat the remaining oil in a small frying pan. Add the mushrooms and shallots, and cook until all the liquid has evaporated. Season to taste with salt and pepper.

Add the bacon, mushrooms, and shallots to the large frying pan. Pour in the wine. Cover and cook over medium heat for 40 minutes.

Blend the flour with the remaining butter to make a paste. Drain the pieces of chicken and put them on a warm serving platter. Add the crème fraîche to the frying pan. Add the butter and flour paste, and thicken over a brisk heat, stirring. Pour this sauce over the chicken and serve immediately.

Makes 6 servings

THE MARIN AGRICULTURAL LAND TRUST

We are very lucky in Marin County, where I live, to have such great organizations as the Marin Agricultural Land Trust (MALT), which was the first land trust in the United States to focus on farmland preservation. It was founded in 1980 by a coalition of ranchers and environmentalists to preserve farmland in Marin County, California. MALT acquires agricultural conservation easements on farmland in voluntary transactions with landowners and also encourages public policies that support and enhance agriculture. It is a model for agricultural land preservation efforts across the nation. So far MALT has permanently protected more than forty thousand acres of land on sixty-two family farms and ranches.

CHICKEN & EGGS

CHICKEN SOUP

3½–4 quarts water

1 free-range chicken, cut into
    8 pieces plus neck

3 medium leeks, cleaned and
    cut into 3-inch lengths
    (white parts and part
    of green only)

1 medium onion, cut into
    quarters

2 small turnips, cut into
    4 wedges each

1 parsnip, peeled and cut into
    pieces

1 bunch fresh parsley

1 tablespoon fresh thyme

2 tablespoons chopped fresh
    dill

1 tablespoon peppercorns

1 teaspoon kosher salt, or to
    taste

4 large carrots, peeled and cut
    into thirds lengthwise

3 ribs celery, cut into 3-inch
    lengths

Pepper to taste

Bring water to a boil in a large soup pot. Add chicken and boil at medium-high heat until cooked through, skimming all the fat that rises to the top. Add the leeks, onions, turnips, parsnip, herbs, peppercorns, and salt and simmer until chicken is falling off the bone. Strain the soup, discarding the vegetables and herbs as you please. Cut the white chicken meat into small pieces and add back into the soup. Stir in the carrots and celery and cook until done. Season to taste with more salt and pepper. Serve hot with cooked noodles, matzo balls, or rice added to it.

Makes 6–8 servings or more

Bob Berner and his dear wife, Barbara, shared their recipe for Chicken Soup. Bob has been MALT's executive director for the past twenty years, and his incredible wife is a board member of our Marin Farmers Markets. I feel like we live in a place where the land is protected, the farmer is cherished, and our food is cultivated with devoted hands. All of this makes for a loving and sustainable community. I'm proud to live in Marin and be a part of all the folks that make this happen.

GALETTES

2 cups buckwheat flour

1 free-range egg

1 teaspoon coarse sea salt

2 cups water

2 teaspoons butter, melted

1 egg yolk

Gruyère cheese, grated

Ham, sliced

Sift the flour into a bowl and form a hole in the middle. Whisk the egg in it. Add salt and gradually add water, mixing the ingredients to form a liquid batter. Then beat vigorously with a mixer. Leave to rest for at least 2 hours, or overnight if possible. Whisk again and add butter.

Heat the pan and grease well with a dollop of butter and egg yolk. This way the galette moves easier in the pan and the buckwheat flavor develops more. Add a ladle of batter and roll the pan so it is distributed over the bottom of the pan. Free the browned edges of the galette from the edge of the pan, turn the galette over, and cook the other side.

What you put in the galette is up to you. The photo shows a slice of ham, some Gruyère cheese, and an egg. Another good combination is figs, prosciutto, and Brie; Brie and apples; or asparagus and Gruyère. When you're satisfied with your fillings, fold the galette over and heat ingredients while cooking the last side of the galette.

Makes 12 servings

These savory crêpes are fun to make, and you can make so many different kinds with a variety of ingredients. Your imagination is your only limitation. These come from my maman's side of the family in Bretagne. I think there are as many crêperies in Bretagne as there are fast-food chains in the United States.

FISH & SEAFOOD

FISH TACOS WITH CREAMY LIME
GUACAMOLE & CABBAGE SLAW

2 Hass avocados—halved,
  pitted, and peeled

¼ cup low-fat sour cream or
  Greek yogurt

1 small jalapeño, seeded and
  thinly sliced

2 tablespoons minced
  red onion

2 tablespoons chopped cilantro

5 tablespoons fresh lime juice,
  divided

Kosher salt and freshly ground
  black pepper

1 small head napa cabbage,
  shredded (about 4 cups)

2 tablespoons vegetable oil,
  plus more for brushing

2 pounds thick red snapper
  fillets with skin, cut crosswise into 10 (2-inch-wide)
  strips

10 (7-inch) flour tortillas,
  warmed

2 medium-size tomatoes, thinly
  sliced

Hot sauce

Lime wedges

Heat the grill to medium heat.

In a medium bowl, mash the avocados, sour cream, jalapeño, onion, cilantro, and 3 tablespoons lime juice. Season the guacamole with salt and pepper, and then press a piece of plastic wrap directly onto the surface of the guacamole; set aside.

In a large bowl, toss the cabbage with the oil and the remaining lime juice. Season with salt and pepper.

Brush the fish with the oil and season with salt and pepper. Grill over moderately high heat until lightly charred and cooked through, about 10 minutes. Transfer the fish to a platter and pull off the skin.

To assemble each taco, spread a dollop of guacamole on a tortilla. Top with a piece of fish, a few tomato slices, and a large spoonful of the cabbage slaw. Serve with the hot sauce and lime wedges on the side.

Makes 10 servings

CRAB & RICE SALAD

FRENCH DRESSING

6 tablespoons oil

2 tablespoons vinegar

2 teaspoons mustard (Dijon
preferred)

A few drops Worcestershire
sauce

Salt and pepper

Chives or green parts of
scallions, chopped

SALAD

2 cups cooked rice

1 tablespoon mayonnaise

½ pound crabmeat

1 cup black pitted olives

Olive oil, enough to coat olives

½ cup pimientos, chopped

Salt and pepper

To make the dressing, whisk all the ingredients together.

To make the salad, stir half of the dressing into the cooked rice. To the remaining dressing, add the mayonnaise and mix with the crab. Coat the olives with a little oil and add to the rice along with the crab mixture and pimiento. Season to taste with salt and pepper, and serve.

Makes 6 servings

SCALLOPS WITH TRUFFLES

24 scallops

Flour

2 tablespoons local butter

2 tablespoons brandy

¾ cup Madeira wine

Salt and pepper

A handful of truffles

I cup crème fraîche, divided

3 free-range egg yolks

Coat the scallops in flour.

Melt the butter in a frying pan, add the scallops, and cook until firm but not browned, about 2 minutes on each side. Add the brandy, wine, salt, and pepper. Boil briskly until the sauce is thick enough to coat the scallops.

Save a little of the truffles for garnish and put the rest in the frying pan with 3 tablespoons crème fraîche. Cook over low heat for 5 to 8 minutes, stirring from time to time.

Mix the egg yolks with the remaining crème. Add this mixture to the pan and stir to thicken over medium heat. Do not allow to boil.

Pour into a serving dish, sprinkle with the reserved truffles, and serve immediately.

Makes 6–8 servings

CRAB & MUSHROOM CRÊPES
WITH SAUCE VELOUTE

2 tablespoons local butter

1 cup fish stock

2 teaspoons flour

$\frac{1}{2}$ cup sherry

Salt and pepper

$\frac{1}{2}$ teaspoon nutmeg

$\frac{1}{2}$ clove garlic

2 free-range egg yolks

$\frac{1}{3}$ cup cream

$\frac{3}{4}$ pound cooked crabmeat

16 crêpes (see Galette recipe
   on page 104)

$\frac{1}{4}$ pound mushroom caps and
   stems, sautéed with garlic

Chopped parsley

Melt butter in a double boiler, add fish stock, and thicken with flour. Season the sauce with sherry, salt, pepper, nutmeg, and garlic. The sauce should cook thoroughly. Fold in the yolks and cream to enrich the sauce, and then fold in the crabmeat. Place a large serving spoonful of crab mixture in the center of each crepe. Fold crêpe around the mixture. Arrange the crêpes in a circular ovenproof dish. Top with mushrooms and chopped parsley. Reheat in the oven at 350 degrees for 5 minutes before serving.

Makes 6–8 servings

SOLE WITH LEMON BUTTER

3 tablespoons flour
Salt and pepper
6 soles, cleaned and skinned
1 1/4 cups vegetable oil
1 cup butter
3 lemons, divided
2 teaspoons chopped fresh
    parsley

Season the flour with salt and pepper. Coat the soles with the seasoned flour.

Heat the oil in the frying pan and fry the soles 2 or 3 at a time, for 8 minutes on each side. Drain the soles as they are cooked and keep hot on a serving dish.

When all the soles are cooked, pour the oil out of the frying pan and wipe the pan clean with a paper towel. Cut the butter into small pieces and heat in the frying pan until it bubbles. Add the juice of 1 lemon, stir well, and pour over the soles. Sprinkle with parsley. Cut the remaining lemons into quarters or slices, and arrange around the fish. Serve immediately.

Makes 6 servings

BAKED SALMON WITH TOMATO,
CUCUMBER, & BASIL BEURRE BLANC

BEURRE BLANC SAUCE

3 tablespoons white wine
vinegar

3 tablespoons dry white wine

2 large shallots, minced

1 cup (2 sticks) chilled unsalted
butter, cut into 16 pieces

½ cup diced, peeled, and
seeded plum tomatoes

½ cup diced, peeled, and
seeded cucumber

Salt and freshly ground white
pepper

¾ cup loosely packed fresh
basil leaves, sliced

SALMON

1 (3–4 pound) salmon fillet,
about 1¼ inches thick

Salt and freshly ground white
pepper

Lemon slices

Fresh basil sprigs

To make the sauce, combine the vinegar, wine, and shallots in a heavy small saucepan. Boil until reduced to 1 tablespoon, about 4 minutes. Remove pan from heat and whisk in 2 pieces of butter. Set pan over low heat and whisk in remaining butter 1 piece at a time, removing pan from heat briefly if drops of melted butter appear. If sauce breaks down at any time during prep, remove from heat and whisk in 2 pieces of cold butter. If sauce thins or turns oily once it is finished, it has become too hot and has broken. To save broken sauce, place 1 teaspoon cold water in a cold bowl, add 1 tablespoon sauce, and whisk until creamy. Gradually whisk in remaining sauce in a slow stream.

Remove sauce from heat and fold in tomatoes and cucumber. Season with salt and pepper. (Sauce can be prepared 1 hour ahead.) Keep warm on top of a double boiler over warm, not hot, water. Mix in basil.

To make the salmon, preheat oven to 350 degrees F.

Line baking pan with foil. Place salmon on foil, skin side down. Sprinkle generously with salt and pepper. Bake until fish is just opaque in center, about 15 minutes.

Transfer salmon to platter. Garnish with lemon slices and basil. Serve spooning the Beurre Blanc sauce over top.

Makes 6–8 servings

CRAB QUICHE WITH MUSHROOMS
& SAUCE BÉCHAMEL

SAUCE BÉCHAMEL

¼ cup butter

⅓ cup flour

1½ cups hot milk

Salt and pepper

Nutmeg

1 free-range egg yolk, beaten

⅓ cup cream

CRAB QUICHE

½ pound butter, divided

1 shallot, chopped

½ cup white wine

½ pound crab, flaked

⅓ cup cognac

1 tablespoon fresh fine herbs, chopped

1 teaspoon fresh aromatic herbs, chopped

⅓ cup sour cream

4 free-range eggs, beaten

⅓ cup grated Parmesan cheese

¼ pound mushrooms, coarsely chopped

1 clove garlic, minced

1 prebaked 9 x 13-inch pastry sheet

To make the sauce, make a white roux by melting the butter in a double boiler or heavy pan over low heat and blending in the flour. Do not allow it to brown. Pour in the hot milk and beat until smooth and well blended. Add the seasonings to taste and cook over hot water on very low heat for 45 minutes to 1 hour. The sauce may be cooled and refrigerated for several days or frozen. When ready to use, heat, adding the egg yolk mixed with the cream at the last moment. Do not allow the sauce to boil after adding the egg yolk and the cream.

To make the quiche, preheat oven to 375 degrees F.

Meanwhile, melt 1 to 1½ tablespoons butter and sauté the shallot in a frying pan. Pour in the wine and ignite. Stir into the Béchamel. Melt 2 to 3 tablespoons butter in another frying pan and sauté the crab. Pour in the cognac and ignite. Add to the Béchamel along with the herbs, sour cream, eggs, and cheese. Now melt 4 tablespoons butter in same pan. When very hot, sauté the mushrooms. Add the garlic and stir into the egg mixture. Pour into the prebaked sheet and loosely cover with tin foil.

Bake for 30 to 35 minutes, or until an inserted knife comes out clean. Bake uncovered for the last 15 minutes.

Makes 6–8

BAKED HALIBUT
WITH RED PEPPER & ONION

2 large red bell peppers, cut
    into 1/4-inch-wide strips
1 medium onion, cut into
    1/4-inch-wide strips
2 tablespoons olive oil, plus
    more for brushing
1 1/2 x 2-inch orange, sliced of
    its rind or peel
1 clove garlic, pressed
4 (1-inch-thick) halibut steaks
1 teaspoon minced fresh thyme
    or 1/4 teaspoon dried,
    crumbled
Freshly ground black pepper
1 tablespoon fresh lemon juice
Lemon wedges
Fresh thyme sprigs

Preheat oven to 400 degrees F.

Combine the bell peppers, onion, oil, and orange in a very large baking dish or ovenproof skillet; stir to coat. Bake until edges of bell peppers and onion begin to brown, stirring occasionally, about 20 minutes.

Mix garlic into vegetable mixture. Push vegetables to one side. Pat fish dry. Brush lightly with oil. Arrange fish in center of dish. Sprinkle with thyme and pepper. Spoon some vegetables on the fish. Bake until fish is opaque in center, about 9 minutes. Drizzle with lemon juice. Divide fish and vegetables among plates. Garnish with lemon wedges and thyme.

Makes 4 servings

ORIGINAL
BLUE OYSTERS

1 tablespoon butter

1 tablespoon chopped onion

2 tablespoons chopped fresh
   parsley

1 clove garlic, finely minced

3 tablespoons unseasoned dry
   breadcrumbs

½ cup (3 ounces) Point Reyes
   Original Blue Cheese
   crumbles

16 small fresh oysters, scrubbed
   clean

Lemon juice (optional)

Preheat oven to 350 degrees F or heat a grill to medium-high.

In a small skillet, melt butter and then add onion. Sauté onion until soft. Add parsley, garlic, and breadcrumbs, and cook about 1 minute. Remove from heat and cool. Stir in cheese crumbles; set aside.

Shuck oysters, discarding the top shell. Keep oyster liqueur in the bottom shell with the oyster. Top each oyster with an equal amount of cheese mixture. Squeeze a small amount of lemon juice on top of each oyster, if desired. Set the oysters, shell side down, either on a baking sheet and bake for 10 to 12 minutes or covered on the grill for 4 to 5 minutes, or until the oyster liqueur just begins to bubble. Serve immediately.

Makes 8 servings

POINT REYES ORIGINAL BLUE

Point Reyes Original Blue, the only blue cheese made in California, is a result of a family changing with the times and circumstances. Bob and Dean Giacomini had four girls. Bob was a dairyman. The girls decided that they didn't want to live on a dairy farm, so they went off to college, got married, had children, and started their lives away from the ranch. Bob and Dean were left with a dairy and no heirs to continue. But Bob had an idea. He invited all his girls for a summer vacation to a cheese farmstead in Wisconsin. Great free vacation, thought the girls. Little did they know that Bob's plan was to change the dairy operation into a cheese-making operation, using his girls to help run the business. Long story short, the girls are back working on the ranch, using their marketing and business degrees to sell some of the best blue cheese in the country. (Photo courtesy of the Giacomini family.)

CRAB CAKES
WITH MELON SALSA

1/4 cup fresh lime juice

2 tablespoons honey

1 tablespoon Dijon mustard
plus 2 teaspoons, divided

2 cups cantaloupe, cubed

1 green bell pepper, diced

1 cup cherry tomatoes,
quartered

1 pound crabmeat

4 scallions, thinly sliced

1/2 teaspoon salt

2 free-range egg whites

1/2 cup plain dry breadcrumbs

2 tablespoons olive oil, divided

In a medium bowl, whisk together the lime juice, honey, and 1 tablespoon mustard. Add the cantaloupe, bell pepper, and tomatoes; toss. Refrigerate salsa until ready to serve.

In a separate bowl, combine the crabmeat, scallions, remaining mustard, and salt. Beat the egg whites until stiff peaks form and gently fold into the crabmeat mixture. Gently shape into 8 patties. Dip the patties in the breadcrumbs.

In a large skillet, heat 1 tablespoon of the oil over medium heat. Add 4 of the crab cakes to the pan, and cook for 2 to 3 minutes per side, or until hot and cooked through. Transfer the cakes to a plate. Repeat with the rest of the oil and patties. Serve the crab cakes with the salsa.

Makes 8 cakes

OYSTER SHOOTER

2½ large tomatoes, peeled,
seeded and diced
½ cup fresh lime juice
¼ cup chipotle sauce or
2 tablespoons puréed
chipotle chiles
1½ tablespoons sugar
1 teaspoon salt
½ teaspoon freshly ground
white pepper
8 drops hot pepper sauce (such
as Tabasco)
18 freshly shucked oysters or
cooked shrimp
1 red onion, finely diced
Fresh cilantro sprigs

Purée the first seven ingredients in a blender and then strain through a fine sieve; refrigerate. May be prepared 1 day ahead.

Place some oysters or several shrimp in 6 shot glasses. Spoon tomato sauce over top. Garnish with red onion and cilantro sprigs and serve.

Makes 6 servings

DRAKES BAY OYSTER COMPANY

At Drakes Bay Oyster Company in Point Reyes, California, oysters grow either as singles or in clusters. The singles are grown as individuals from the larval stage. The single oysters are produced in the indoor hatchery located on farm and are then moved to the growing area in mesh bags to resist predation from Bat Rays. Clusters are created by setting many larvae on shells saved from the shucking and packing operation. These "mother" shells containing the oyster spat (baby oysters) are then strung together on wires and suspended in Drakes Estero. These cluster oysters are usually shucked and packed in jars in California's last oyster cannery, located on farm at Drakes Bay Oyster Company.

Historically and currently, the shellfish species produced in the Drake's Estero include

Olympia Oysters, Pacific Oysters, Kumamoto Oysters, Manila Clams, and Purple Hinged Rock Scallops. These shellfish continue to be produced as "singles" and are sold live in shell as well as shucked and packed in various sized containers. The water temperature of Drakes Estero is too cold for the non-native oysters to spawn on their own, so they must be seeded by hand, eliminating the risk of unintended invasion. The Drakes Bay Oyster Farm produces its own shellfish seed. This advanced hatchery technique allows the farm to curtail the purchasing of seed (small shellfish) from producers in other waters, thus lessening the risk of introducing other contaminates and non-native species to the ocean.

SAUCES & MARINADES

SAUCE BORDELAISE

1 cup red wine

1–2 shallots, finely chopped

4 cloves garlic, minced

½ teaspoon aromatic herbs
(thyme, sage, marjoram, etc.)

1 teaspoon chopped parsley

1 cup beef stock, plus some for
thinning

1 teaspoon beef extract

4 tablespoons butter or
margarine

2–3 tablespoons flour

1 lemon, juiced

In a saucepan, combine the wine, shallots, garlic, and herbs. Reduce until only ¾ cup is left. Add the beef stock and beef extract; keep warm.

Meanwhile, melt the butter in the top of a double boiler over medium heat. Let the butter brown slightly before stirring in the flour. Let the mixture cook together until a deep brown color is attained. Slowly add the wine mixture and lemon juice. Cover and cook over low heat for at least 25 minutes. Thin the sauce with a little more stock before serving.

Makes about 2 cups

HOLLANDAISE SAUCE

4 free-range egg yolks

2 teaspoons lemon juice

Salt and pepper

½ cup butter, cut in small
   pieces

Beat the egg yolks thoroughly with the lemon juice, salt, and pepper. Put mixture in the top of a double boiler over hot, not boiling, water with the stove on medium heat. Stir the mixture constantly until it starts to thicken slightly. Add the butter and beat the sauce until it is the consistency of mayonnaise. Up to ¼ cup more butter can be incorporated, if desired, but it is better to have less than risk separating the sauce. Remove the sauce from the heat and serve. It will keep warm for half an hour on the side of the stove.

Makes 4 cups

CABERNET PEPPERCORN SAUCE

1 cup chopped white
   mushrooms

½ cup chopped shallots

3 tablespoons black peppercorns

¼ cup olive oil

½ cup red wine, preferably
   Cabernet

2 quarts demi-glace

½ cup heavy cream

1 tablespoon beef base

Cornstarch and cold water,
   as needed

Salt and pepper

Sauté mushrooms, shallots, and peppercorns in oil in a sauce-pan over medium heat. When shallots are tender, deglaze with wine and reduce by two-thirds. Whisk together the reduction and demi-glace until smooth. Whisk in the cream and beef base. Combine a few teaspoons of cornstarch (or more as needed) with a little cold water to make a slurry. (Definition: A thickening mixture made up of flour or cornstarch and water.) Add slurry to the sauce to thicken; cook for 1 minute and then remove from the heat. Season with salt and pepper.

Makes 3 cups

BÉARNAISE SAUCE

¼ cup vinegar

¼ cup dry white wine (Chablis or Sauterne)

2 shallots, chopped

1 tablespoon tarragon

2 teaspoons minced parsley

2 teaspoons minced chives

Salt and pepper

3 free-range egg yolks, beaten

½ cup butter, cut into small pieces

In the top of a double boiler, boil vinegar and wine with the shallots, tarragon, parsley, chives, salt, and pepper until the liquid has been reduced to 2 to 3 tablespoons. Put over hot, not boiling, water and add egg yolks and stir until slightly thickened. Beat in butter until it is the consistency of mayonnaise. Up to ¼ cup more butter can be incorporated, if desired, but it is better to have less than risk separating the sauce. Remove the sauce from the heat and serve. It will keep warm for half an hour on the side of the stove.

Makes 1 cup

COFFEE & CHILE MARINADE

6 cups strong brewed coffee, room temperature (don't use decaf or instant)
1 cup soy sauce
7 cloves garlic, minced
1/2 ounce crushed chile peppers (optional)

Combine all the ingredients in a large bowl. Add beef cut of your choice, pushing it down so it is well immersed in the liquid. Cover the bowl with plastic wrap and refrigerate for 2 to 12 hours.

Makes 6 cups

BLUE CHEESE STEAK TOPPER

3/4 cup Point Reyes Blue Cheese crumbles
2 tablespoons butter, softened
1 tablespoon chopped fresh flat-leaf parsley

Blend together the blue cheese and butter in a small bowl until creamy. Equally divide blue cheese mixture over cooked steaks. Keep steaks on grill for 30 seconds or until butter melts. Garnish with parsley.

Makes 3/4 cup

VEGETABLES

ROASTED SEASONAL HARVEST VEGETABLES

3 tablespoons olive oil

6 cloves garlic, sliced

3 cups 1-inch chunks butternut squash

10 ounces Brussels sprouts, trimmed and halved lengthwise

8 ounces fresh shiitake mushrooms, stemmed and thickly sliced

2 large red apples, unpeeled and cut into 1-inch chunks

1/4 cup oil-packed sun-dried tomatoes, drained and thinly sliced

1 teaspoon minced rosemary

1/2 teaspoon salt

1/4 cup grated Parmesan cheese

Preheat oven to 400 degrees F.

In a large roasting pan, combine the oil and garlic. Heat for 3 minutes in oven. Add the squash, Brussels sprouts, mushrooms, apples, tomatoes, rosemary, and salt; toss.

Roast for 35 minutes, or until the vegetables are tender, tossing every 10 minutes. Sprinkle the Parmesan over the vegetables and roast for 5 minutes more.

Have fun with this dish and try all sorts of seasoning combinations based on what you like.

Makes 4 servings

My grandmother had an ABC of Cooking book, and there were no measurements, only what was in the dish. The individual chef decides according to their own taste the quantities they want in the dish. For example, a recipe for stew would read, "Stew: Carrots, meat, potatoes, peas, mushrooms, red wine, and a little flour or cornstarch." Then you the chef would decide if you wanted more carrots than potatoes, etc. That's how my mom taught me most of her recipes. The conversation would always start with, "AHHHHH Brigitte, I don't know, I put a little of this and a little of that, and I make stew. Just start, and it will come." She was right. It did come. From taste and trial and error, I started making recipes of my own. (That, by the way, is the recipe for my stew. I use Madeira wine.)

CAULIFLOWER WITH CHEESE SAUCE

1 large cauliflower
¼ cup butter, divided
6 tablespoons flour
1 cup crème fraîche
1 cup grated Gruyère or
    Swiss cheese
Grated nutmeg
Salt and pepper

Preheat oven to 375 degrees F.

Remove the outer leaves from the cauliflower. Cut into the hard stem and separate the cauliflower into large florets.

In a saucepan, bring some salted water to a boil. Add the cauliflower and the rest of the butter and bring back to a boil. Lower the heat and simmer gently without a lid for 10 to 15 minutes. Pierce the cauliflower with the blade of a knife. The florets should be cooked but still firm.

Meanwhile, melt 3 tablespoons butter in a saucepan, add the flour, and stir until it is absorbed. Gradually stir in the crème fraîche and cook, stirring, until thickened. Flavor with two-thirds of the grated cheese, a pinch of nutmeg, salt, and pepper; sprinkle the dish with the rest of the cheese.

Makes 4 servings

AVOCADO & ZUCCHINI SALAD

3 cups shredded zucchini

1 medium-size firm ripe
    avocado

1 cup arugula or watercress
    sprigs, rinsed and crisped

¼ cup olive oil

1 lemon, juiced

Salt and pepper

8 Greek olives (optional)

Place zucchini in a wide shallow bowl. Peel, pit, and slice the avocado. Arrange avocado and arugula over zucchini.

In a small bowl, combine oil and lemon juice; season to taste with salt and pepper, and then mix well. Pour dressing over salad and mix lightly. Garnish with olives, if desired.

Makes 4 servings

BELGIUM ENDIVES

8 large endives

1 teaspoon sugar

1/2 teaspoon salt

16 slices ham

20 slices Swiss or
  Gruyère cheese

2 tablespoons organic milk

1 tablespoon butter

Place the endives in a pot, cover with water, and add the sugar and salt. Cook over medium heat for 20 to 25 minutes; drain well. Cut endives in half; set aside.

Preheat oven to 350 degrees F.

Place a slice of ham on an endive half; place a slice of cheese on top then roll and place in a glass rectangular baking dish; repeat. Once the pan is full of the rolled endives, take the rest of the cheese and either grate or cut into thin slices and spread over top. Sprinkle the milk over the cheese and dice the butter and sprinkle over top as well.

Bake for about 15 to 20 minutes, or until everything is melted and hot.

Makes 8 servings

ROASTED ROSEMARY BUTTERNUT SQUASH & SHALLOTS

1 large butternut squash

4 medium shallots

2 tablespoons extra virgin
    olive oil

1 teaspoon chopped fresh
    rosemary

1 teaspoon kosher salt

1/2 teaspoon granulated sugar

1/2 teaspoon freshly ground
    black pepper

With a rack in the center of the oven, preheat to 450 degrees F.

Square off ends and cut squash in two just above bulbous part. Stand sections on flat ends and use sharp knife (or vegetable peeler) to remove outer peel, slicing from top to bottom. Cut rounded end in half lengthwise and scoop out seeds. Cut squash into uniform 3/4-inch cubes to make about 3 cups.

Put squash on a heavy-duty rimmed baking sheet. Peel and quarter each shallot and add to squash. Drizzle oil over vegetables; toss to coat. Sprinkle rosemary, salt, sugar, and pepper over squash; toss to coat. Distribute vegetables evenly on baking sheet. Roast for 20 minutes. Stir and then continue roasting until vegetables are tender and lightly browned, 10 to 15 minutes more. Before serving, taste and season with more salt if needed.

Makes 4 servings

BUTTON MUSHROOMS BAKED IN CREAM

2 pounds button mushrooms, cleaned, trimmed, and thinly sliced

1 lemon, juiced

¼ cup butter, divided

2 shallots, peeled and finely chopped

1 clove garlic, cut in half

¾ cup organic crème fraîche

⅔ cup organic milk

1 free-range egg yolk

1 tablespoon cornstarch or potato starch

Salt and pepper

Preheat oven to 400 degrees F.

Sprinkle mushrooms with a little lemon juice. Melt three-quarters of the butter in a frying pan and add the mushrooms and shallots. Cook until the liquid from the mushrooms has evaporated, stirring frequently. Do not allow to dry out completely.

Rub a gratin dish with the garlic clove and discard.

Mix the crème fraîche in a bowl with the milk, egg yolk, and cornstarch or potato starch. Season with salt and pepper.

Put the mushrooms and shallots into the gratin dish and pour the mixture of egg, flour, and crème fraîche over top. Dot with the remaining butter. Bake for 30 minutes without allowing the mixture to boil.

Makes 6 servings

GLAZED CARROTS
& APRICOTS

4 pounds carrots, peeled,
    washed, and chopped
½ cup butter
2 tablespoons sugar
10 apricots
Salt and pepper

Trim carrots into the your favorite shape, keeping them equal
lengths.

Melt butter in a heavy-bottomed saucepan and add the carrots,
sugar, apricots, salt, and pepper. Cover with water.

Cook, uncovered, over a gentle heat for 20 to 30 minutes, or
until the water has evaporated and the carrots are coated with the
golden syrupy liquid.

Makes 6 servings

SWEET & SOUR CARROTS

2 pounds small or baby carrots,
    peeled and trimmed

2 tablespoons extra virgin
    olive oil

Salt

1/2 cup fresh orange juice

1/4 cup fresh lemon juice

1/4 cup elderflower cordial

1 tablespoon pink peppercorns,
    coarsely ground in a mortar

2 tablespoons unsalted butter

2 tablespoons chopped cilantro

Arrange the carrots in a single layer in a skillet just large enough to hold them. Add the oil, a pinch of salt, and just enough water to cover. Simmer over moderate heat until the carrots are tender, about 45 minutes.

Add the orange and lemon juices, elderflower cordial, and peppercorns to the saucepan and simmer for 3 minutes.

Remove the pan from heat and swirl in the butter. Stir in the cilantro, season with salt, and serve.

Makes 6 servings

SAUTÉED BABY ARTICHOKES

2 pounds baby artichokes,
    washed
Lemon juice or vinegar
¼ cup butter
½ clove garlic
Salt and pepper

Snap off the lower petals of the artichoke until you reach the yellow-green core. Use a knife and cut off the top half-inch of the baby artichoke, or just below the green tips of the petals. To preserve the color, immediately soak in water with lemon or vinegar until you are ready to cook. Quarter the artichoke and place in a skillet, coated lightly with butter and the garlic, salt, and pepper. Cover skillet and sauté artichokes slowly over medium-high heat for about 5 minutes, or until they brown to your liking.

Makes 4 servings

SPINACH SOUFFLÉ

3 pounds fresh spinach, washed
    and stemmed
Salt
¼ cup butter
¼ cup flour
2½ cups organic milk
Pepper
Freshly grated nutmeg
½ cup grated Gruyère or
    Swiss cheese
4 free-range eggs, yolks and
    whites separated

Put spinach in a large saucepan with a large pinch of salt. Cook over medium heat for 8 minutes; drain well. Leave to cool a little and then press the leaves between the palms of your hands to extract all the water. Finely chop the spinach and set aside.

Preheat oven to 425 degrees F.

Melt the butter in a saucepan, add the flour, and stir until it has been absorbed. Gradually stir in the milk and cook, stirring, until thickened. Season with salt and pepper, and add a little nutmeg and the grated cheese.

Add 2 tablespoons of the sauce to the egg yolks and beat well. Stir in the rest of the sauce. Add the spinach.

Beat the egg whites until they are stiff and carefully fold them into the spinach mixture.

Pour into a buttered 8-inch soufflé dish to fill it three-quarters full. Bake for 30 minutes without opening the oven door. Then increase the oven temperature to 450 degrees F and bake for another 5 minutes. Serve immediately.

Makes 4–6 servings

WINTER SQUASH GRATIN

4 cups peeled kabocha squash,
butternut squash, or pumpkin, cut into 1-inch cubes

½ teaspoon salt

2 teaspoons butter

½ cup thinly sliced onion

1¾ cups skim milk

2½ tablespoons flour

½ cup grated fontinella cheese

⅛ teaspoon nutmeg

⅛ teaspoon freshly ground
pepper

1 slice white bread

1 teaspoon chopped fresh
parsley

1 clove garlic, minced

Preheat over to 400 degrees F.

Place squash and salt in a single layer on a baking sheet coated
with nonstick spray. Bake squash for 25 minutes, or until tender.

Melt butter in a large nonstick skillet over medium heat. Add
onion and sauté until tender.

Whisk milk and flour together until combined and add to skillet.
Bring to a boil and then cook for 1 minute, stirring constantly.
Remove from heat and stir in cheese, nutmeg, and pepper, stirring
constantly until cheese melts.

Gently stir in squash and pour mixture into a greased baking
dish, about 1-quart size.

Place bread in a food processor and pulse into coarse crumbs,
measuring about ⅔ cup. Add parsley and garlic, pulsing once or
twice to combine. Sprinkle bread mixture over the squash. Bake
for 20 minutes, or until golden brown.

Makes 4–6 servings

EGGPLANT PARMIGIANA

2 tablespoons oil

2 large eggplants, peeled and
    sliced ¼ inch thick

All-purpose flour

4 free-range eggs

Italian seasoned breadcrumbs

6 cups marinara sauce (optional
    ½ pound sautéed mush-
    rooms added into sauce)

8 ounces mozzarella, sliced

½ cup grated Romano cheese

Preheat oven to 350 degrees F.

Heat oil in a large pan, Dutch oven, or deep fryer. Coat each side of the eggplant with flour.

In a separate bowl, beat the eggs and dip the eggplant in the egg to coat both sides. Then coat each slice with breadcrumbs.

In batches, place the eggplant in the hot oil and fry until golden brown. If you use a deep fryer, leave in for 2 to 3 minutes.

In a 9 x 13-inch pan, make layers starting with marinara sauce on the bottom of the pan, then a layer of eggplant slices, then a little more sauce, and then mozzarella slices and Romano cheese. Continue layering until you reach the top of the pan, topping off with sauce, mozzarella, and Romano. Place the casserole in the oven and cook for 20 to 25 minutes. Let sit for 5 minutes before serving.

Makes 6–8 servings

LINGUINE
WITH ARTICHOKES

2 lemons, divided

3 large artichokes

1 tablespoon olive oil

2 ounces pancetta, chopped

1 cup chopped onion

2 slices cooked bacon, chopped

1 tablespoon chopped garlic

1/2 teaspoon salt

3 tablespoons chopped fresh
   flat-leaf parsley, divided

1 cup chicken broth

1/2 cup white wine

1 pound linguine, cooked
   according to package
   directions

1/2 cup grated fresh Parmesan
   cheese

1/4 teaspoon black pepper

Fill a bowl with cold water and then squeeze juice from 1 lemon into bowl.

Trim artichoke stems to 1 inch and peel. Bend back tough outer petals until they snap off near base and a layer of tender yellow petals is exposed. Discard outer petals. Cut off top quarter of each artichoke. With a knife, peel outer dark green layer from base and stem. Halve artichokes. Remove purple fuzzy centers. Rub all sides with remaining lemon halves; place artichokes in water. Thinly slice artichoke halves. Squeeze juice from lemons over slices.

Heat oil in a Dutch oven. Add pancetta and cook until it begins to brown. Add onion, bacon, garlic, and salt; cook until onions soften. Stir in artichoke slices and 2 tablespoons parsley. Add broth and wine; bring to a boil. Place a sheet of waxed paper directly on top of artichokes and then cover pan with lid. Simmer artichokes until tender, about 15 minutes.

Toss hot pasta with artichokes and remaining parsley. Top with Parmesan cheese and pepper.

Makes 4 servings

ASPARAGUS & GRILLED SHIITAKE WITH SOY VINAIGRETTE

2 tablespoons extra virgin olive oil, plus more for drizzling

2 tablespoons soy sauce

1 tablespoon fresh lemon juice

1 tablespoon rice vinegar

2 tablespoons chopped tarragon

Salt and freshly ground pepper

1 ½ pounds shiitake mushrooms, stemmed

2 pounds thin asparagus

Heat a grill to medium heat.

In a small bowl, mix 2 tablespoons oil with the soy sauce, lemon juice, vinegar, and tarragon. Season with salt and pepper.

Brush the mushrooms with 2 tablespoons of the soy vinaigrette; season with salt and pepper. Grill over moderate heat, turning once, until just tender, about 6 minutes. Transfer the mushrooms to a bowl; cut any large ones into quarters. Add 4 tablespoons of the soy vinaigrette and toss to coat.

Bring a large skillet of salted water to a boil. Fill a large bowl with ice water. Add the asparagus to the skillet and cook until crisp-tender, about 3 minutes. Transfer to the ice water to cool. Drain and pat dry with paper towels.

Snap the asparagus bottoms off and then arrange the asparagus on a platter. Drizzle with olive oil and season with salt and pepper. Spoon the mushrooms over the asparagus, drizzle the remaining vinaigrette on top, and serve.

Makes 8–10 servings

RED, WHITE, & BLUE POTATO SALAD

1 pound small red potatoes,
   peeled
1 pound small white potatoes,
   peeled
1 pound small blue potatoes,
   peeled
1/4 cup olive oil
2 tablespoons chopped fresh
   basil
2 tablespoons chopped fresh
   rosemary
1 large red onion, chopped
2 to 3 green onions, chopped
5 to 6 gherkin pickles, chopped
1/4 cup chopped black olives
Mayonnaise to taste
Brown and yellow mustard
   to taste
Salt and pepper to taste
2 tablespoons chopped fresh
   parsley

In a 5- or 6-quart pan, boil potatoes until just tender when pierced; drain and cut into cubes. While still warm, toss potatoes with oil, basil, and rosemary. Stir in onions, pickles, and olives. Add mayonnaise and mustards according to desired consistency. Season with salt and pepper. You may also stir in a couple splashes of pickle juice. Garnish the top of the salad with parsley.

Makes 6–8 servings

Beverly Fox's Red, White, & Blue Potato Salad was a favorite recipe from her tenure as a deli owner. It tastes even better these days with the dry-farmed potatoes her husband David Little is digging up at Little Organic Farm just outside of Petaluma, CA.

HOT RED BELL PEPPER JELLY

At our Marin Farmers Market, we have a producer named Leon Day, quite a character, who used to drive Jerry Garcia's car for him. But more importantly, he makes a red pepper sauce that you *can spread on top of the Grilled Portobello (page 150) or any sandwich. I like it plain with crackers and a little dab of goat cheese.*

GRILLED PORTOBELLO,
BELL PEPPER, & GOAT CHEESE SANDWICHES

¼ cup balsamic vinegar

1 tablespoon olive oil

1 clove garlic, minced

1 red bell pepper, halved
   and seeded

4 (4-inch) Portobello
   mushroom caps

⅓ cup chopped fresh basil

¼ teaspoon salt

¼ teaspoon freshly ground
   black pepper

4 Kaiser rolls or whatever
   you prefer

½ cup soft goat cheese

Preheat a grill to medium heat.

Combine vinegar, oil, and garlic in a large bowl. Add bell pepper and mushrooms; toss gently to coat. Remove vegetables from vinegar mixture; discard mixture.

Place bell pepper and mushrooms on a grill rack coated with cooking spray; grill 4 minutes on each side. Remove vegetables from grill and cool slightly. Cut bell peppers into thin strips. Combine peppers, basil, salt, and pepper in a small bowl.

Cut rolls in half horizontally and spread goat cheese evenly over cut sides of rolls. Arrange a mushroom cap on bottom half of each roll and then top with about ⅓ cup pepper mixture and the top half of roll.

Place sandwich on grill coated with cooking spray. Place a cast-iron skillet on top of sandwich; press gently to flatten. Grill 3 minutes on each side or until bread is toasted, leaving skillet on top of sandwich while it cooks. Repeat with remaining sandwiches.

Makes 4 sandwiches

FRUITS

GRILLED NECTARINE SALAD

4 nectarines, slightly under ripe,
   halved and pitted
1 teaspoon extra virgin olive oil
¼ pound goat cheese
2 tablespoons honey
8 basil leaves, sliced into thin
   ribbons
¼ cup pine nuts, toasted
Coarsely ground black pepper

Heat grill to medium heat.

Brush cut side of the nectarines with oil and place on the grill, cut side down. Grill for 2 to 3 minutes, or until golden brown and caramelized. Turn over and grill for 1 to 2 minutes, or until slightly soft. Remove from the grill and top each half with 1 tablespoon goat cheese. Drizzle with honey and garnish with basil, pine nuts, and a sprinkling of black pepper.

Makes 4 servings

SPINACH-TANGERINE SALAD

6 cups baby spinach leaves
12 tangerines, peeled and
   sectioned
1 cup walnut or pecan pieces
1 bunch green onions, sliced
   crosswise
1 cup sliced water chestnuts

DRESSING

3 tablespoons extra virgin
   olive oil
1 cup fresh lemon or lime juice
1 tablespoon Dijon mustard

Place all the salad ingredients in a bowl. Stir all the dressing ingredients together and then toss with the salad and serve.

Makes 4–6 servings

SWEET & SAVORY BERRY SALAD

1 small basket fresh strawberries or blackberries
1/4 cup balsamic vinegar
Freshly ground black pepper

Toss berries with vinegar and then sprinkle them with a grind or two of pepper.

Makes 4 servings

RED ONION & BLOOD ORANGE SALAD

2–3 large juicy blood oranges,
   peeled and thinly sliced
1 small red onion, finely chopped
1 dash red wine vinegar
1 dash extra virgin olive oil
1 teaspoon caster sugar
Whole pink peppercorns

Place oranges on a serving tray. Cover with onion and then drizzle with vinegar and oil. Season with sugar and sprinkle some pink peppercorns over top.

Makes 4–6 servings

WATERMELON SALAD

1 large watermelon
1/2 cup fruit-flavored olive oil
Sea salt
Fresh mint or basil, shredded

Cut and cube the watermelon. Sprinkle watermelon with oil, salt, and mint or basil.

Makes 6 servings

FAR WITH PRUNES

24 prunes

1 large tablespoon rum

1 cup flour, sifted

½ cup sugar

Salt

6 free-range eggs

4 cups organic milk, lukewarm

1 tablespoon salted butter,
   melted

Soak prunes in rum for 30 minutes.

Preheat oven to 450 degrees F.

Mix the flour with the sugar and a pinch of salt, and then make a hole in the middle. Add the eggs and work everything into a smooth dough. Slowly add milk and butter.

Generously grease a baking pan with butter. Spread the prunes on the bottom of the pan and then pour the cake batter on top. Dough should not be too runny.

Bake for 10 minutes and then lower the temperature to 350 degrees F. Serve cold or lukewarm with a glass of milk or sweet cider.

Makes 6 servings

MOM'S PEACH COBBLER

FILLING

2½ pounds peaches, cut into slices

2 tablespoons butter

¾ cup sugar

½ teaspoon nutmeg

2 tablespoons cornstarch (a little more if the peaches are extra ripe)

DOUGH

1 cup flour

2 tablespoons sugar

1½ teaspoons baking powder

Salt

¼ cup butter

1 free-range egg

¼ cup organic milk

To make the filling, layer the peach slices in the bottom of a shallow baking dish and dot with butter.

In a saucepan, mix together the sugar, 2 tablespoons water, nutmeg, and cornstarch, and boil for 1 minute.

To make the dough, preheat oven to 425 degrees F.

Sift the flour, sugar, baking powder, and a pinch of salt into a mixing bowl. Add butter and cut in with a pastry cutter. Beat the egg and add to the milk. Add liquid mixture to dry mixture and stir with about twenty-five strokes. Turn dough onto floured wax paper, knead, and roll out to ¼ inch thickness. Pour the filling over the peaches and layer the dough over the top. Using a knife, gently slice a few holes in the top. (You can also clump the dough on top of the filling like biscuits.)

Bake for about 20 minutes and serve warm.

Makes 6–8 servings

Debra Santana's mom, Jo Francis King, loved using fresh ingredients as much as possible. When farmers markets first sprang up in Marin County, Debra and her mom traveled to them together to pick fresh fruits and vegetables. Debra offered this recipe in memory of her mother, who passed away in 2006. She likes to think of it as Mom's PEACE Cobbler, since her mom always wanted peace in everyone's life and in our world. Adding a scoop of vanilla ice cream from Straus Family Creamery makes it a little bit of heaven.

APRICOT UPSIDE DOWN CAKE

1/2 cup light brown sugar

12 tablespoons butter, at room
temperature, divided

2 pounds apricots, peeled
and halved

2 1/4 cups flour

1 1/2 teaspoons baking soda

1/4 teaspoon salt

1/2 teaspoon ground nutmeg

1 cup granulated sugar

1 free-range egg

1 teaspoon vanilla extract

1 1/2 cups sour cream

Preheat oven to 350 degrees F.

Cook brown sugar in 5 tablespoons butter in a 10-inch oven-proof frying pan until dissolved. Turn off the heat; arrange apricots, cut sides up, in pan. Combine flour, baking soda, salt, nutmeg, and sugar. Beat in egg and vanilla. Stir in flour mixture by thirds, alternating with sour cream. Spread over apricots and bake until toothpick inserted in center comes out clean, about 50 to 55 minutes.

Makes 8 servings

FRUIT KABOBS
WITH WARM CHOCOLATE SAUCE

5 apricots, pitted and quartered

1/4 pound cherries, pitted and
halved

3 apples, cut into eighths
(Crispin, Braeburn, Empire,
Fuji, Gala, Ginger Gold, and
Pink Lady are a few of the
sweeter varieties that are
good to eat freshly cut)

6 skewers

1 tablespoon butter

WARM
CHOCOLATE SAUCE

6 ounces semisweet chocolate

3 tablespoons butter

1 cup water

1 cup sugar

1 1/2 teaspoons vanilla

Preheat grill to medium heat or use oven broiler.

Thread the fruits onto 6 skewers. Melt the butter and brush on the fruit. Grill or broil the kabobs for about 8 minutes, turning several times. Serve with Warm Chocolate Sauce.

To make the sauce, melt the chocolate and butter together over low heat. Gradually add the water, stirring until smooth. Stir in the sugar and vanilla. Bring to a boil and cook about 5 to 7 minutes without stirring, or until sauce is thick enough to lightly coat a spoon.

Makes 6 servings

APPLE TART

1 1/4 cups flour

2 tablespoons sugar

1/2 teaspoon salt

1 teaspoon baking powder

1/2 cup butter

2 tablespoons organic milk

1 free-range egg

6–10 favorite baking apples,
    peeled and cut into 1/4-inch
    slices

TOPPING

3/4 cup sugar

2 tablespoons butter

2 tablespoons flour

Cinnamon (optional)

1/2 pint whipping cream,
    whipped and sweetened
    according to package
    directions

Mix together all the dry ingredients and butter until it becomes a cornmeal texture.

Whisk together the milk and egg, and add to the "cornmeal." Press into a half sheet pan. Overlay the apples in rows on top of the crust.

Preheat oven to 375 degrees F.

To the make the topping, mix the sugar, butter, flour, and cinnamon. Mix until combined but stop before it starts to clump together. Spread mixture over the apples. Bake until it takes on a deep caramel color, about 10 minutes. Dollop each slice with whipped cream and serve warm.

Makes 6–8 servings

Manka's Inverness Lodge is an incredible secret of West Marin. They had a fire not too long ago, and we hope they will rebuild, but brunch is still available. Margaret Grade served this dessert at a Farm Bureau lunch I went to at Corda's Ranch and was kind enough to share the recipe with all the guests.

BLUEBERRY-ORANGE TARTINE

1½ cups flour

⅓ cup powdered sugar

2 teaspoons grated orange zest

½ teaspoon baking powder

½ teaspoon salt

¼ cup plus 3 tablespoons butter

2 tablespoons freshly squeezed orange juice, plus ¼ cup

2 small baskets blueberries

8 tablespoons granulated sugar

3 tablespoons cornstarch

In a large bowl, stir together the flour, powdered sugar, orange zest, baking powder, and salt. Add the butter and 2 tablespoons orange juice, and stir until the mixture comes together. Transfer the dough to a lightly floured cutting board or countertop and knead ten times, or until the dough forms a ball. Flatten into a disk, wrap in plastic wrap, and let sit for 30 minutes at room temperature.

Preheat oven to 350 degrees F.

With your fingertips, gently press the dough onto the bottom and sides of a 9-inch tart pan with a removable bottom. Prick the bottom of the shell with a fork and line the pan with foil on top of the crust. Fill the foil with dried beans or rice to hold it in place. Bake for 15 minutes. Remove the foil and beans, and bake the shell for 10 minutes more, or until golden brown. Cool on a wire rack.

Meanwhile, in a saucepan, combine the blueberries, remaining orange juice, granulated sugar, and cornstarch. Stir cornstarch mixture into berries and cook for 2 minutes, or until the berry mixture is thick. Cool the blueberry mixture to room temperature and then spoon into the baked shell. Chill tart for 1 hour before serving.

Makes 8 servings

RASPBERRY SANTA ROSA PLUM BUTTER

1½ pounds Santa Rosa plums,
    pitted and quartered
1 basket raspberries
½ cup water
1½ cups sugar
1 tablespoon fresh lemon juice

Bring the first three ingredients to a boil in a heavy medium-size saucepan. Reduce heat and simmer until plums are very tender, about 10 minutes.

Purée fruit mixture in a blender. Return to the same saucepan. Add sugar and lemon juice, and stir until sugar dissolves. Cook 18 minutes over medium-high heat, stirring constantly, or until mixture is thick and glossy. Pour into a bowl and cool completely. Cover and refrigerate overnight.

Makes 4 cups

PEAR
TART

2 cups water

1 cup sugar

1 pound pears

1 pastry sheet

1 (8-ounce) jar orange
  marmalade

1 lemon, juiced

Roasted almonds, chopped

½ pint whipping cream,
  whipped and sweetened
  with powdered sugar
  to taste

Preheat oven to 350 degrees F.

Mix the water and sugar to make a light syrup and then heat to just below the boiling point. Poach the pears in the syrup for 10 minutes. Remove from syrup and allow to cool.

Roll out the pastry sheet, line a pie plate with it, cover it with foil, and put a weight on the foil. Bake for 15 minutes.

Remove the weight and the foil.

Spread half of the orange marmalade in a thin layer on the bottom of the crust. Cut the poached pears into quarters and arrange over the marmalade. Melt the other half of the orange marmalade with the lemon juice and glaze the pears with it. Sprinkle the tart with chopped roasted almonds. Decorate tart with whipped cream.

Makes 8 servings

PEARS WITH SABAYON

3–4 free-range egg yolks

1/3 cup white wine or sherry

4 tablespoons sugar

4 pears, poached

Mix together the egg yolks, wine or sherry, and sugar in the top of a double boiler over hot water. Beat until it becomes thick and forms a ribbon when dropped from the beater.

Arrange the pears in a deep dish and pour the sabayon over top. Serve immediately.

Makes 4 servings

FRESH PEACH SALSA

2 cups diced fresh peaches
   (pitted)

1 cup chopped red bell peppers
   (cored)

2 cups chopped cucumber
   (peeled and seeded)

1/4 cup sliced green onion

1 jalapeño, finely chopped

2 tablespoons honey

2 1/2 tablespoons freshly
   squeezed lime juice

1 tablespoon finely chopped
   fresh cilantro

Mix all the ingredients together and chill. Serve with chips, salmon, or chicken.

Makes 3 cups

GRILLED PEACHES, NECTARINES, & PLUMS

4 peaches, nectarines, and/or
    plums, quartered
Butter, melted

Clean grill and then heat to low heat.

Brush the fruit with melted butter and then grill for 6 to 10 minutes, or until fruit is softened. Serve as a side dish or on a cheese plate alongside some blue or goat cheese.

Makes 4 servings

Eddie Chavez has been bringing the sweetest stone fruit (fruit with a pit inside) to the farmers markets for nearly 25 years. His favorite recipes are the ones with the most fruit in them. He encourages his customers to keep the recipe simple, and to let the fruit speak for itself.

ICED MELON
WITH PORT WINE

3 cold ripe cantaloupes
¾ cup Port wine

Cut each melon in half and remove the seeds 30 minutes before serving.

Pour 2 tablespoons of port wine into each melon half and return melons to the refrigerator to marinate for 30 minutes. Serve.

Makes 6 servings

STRAWBERRIES & BURGUNDY

2 small baskets organic straw-
    berries, washed, stemmed,
    and quartered
2 cups burgundy
1 cup sugar

Evenly divide the strawberries in 6 to 8 bowls. Combine the burgundy and sugar in a separate bowl and then ladle over strawberries. Serve cold or at room temperature.

Makes 6–8 servings

DESSERTS

ZUCCHINI CAKE
WITH LEMON ICING

¼ cup extra virgin olive oil

2 large free-range eggs

¾ cup granulated sugar

1 teaspoon lemon zest

4 tablespoons fresh lemon
    juice, divided

¼ cup low-fat lemon or
    vanilla yogurt

1½ cups all-purpose flour

½ teaspoon baking soda

1 teaspoon baking powder

¼ teaspoon salt

1 cup shredded zucchini

1 cup chopped almonds or
    walnuts

1 cup powdered sugar

Preheat oven to 350 degrees F.

Coat an 8-inch cake pan lightly with butter.

Whisk oil and eggs in a large bowl. Beat in sugar, zest, 2 tablespoons lemon juice, and yogurt. Add flour, baking soda, baking powder, and salt; mix until combined. Stir in zucchini and
almonds. Pour batter into prepared pan.

Bake on center oven rack 25 minutes, or until toothpick inserted
in center comes out clean. Cool in pan 10 minutes. Then transfer
to a cooling rack to cool completely.

Stir sugar and 2 tablespoons lemon juice in small bowl until
smooth. Pour over cake and spread to edges.

Makes 8–10 servings

CRÈME ANGLAISE

1 quart organic milk
1 vanilla bean (get a real vanilla
    bean if you can; otherwise
    use vanilla extract.)
Salt
8–10 free-range egg yolks
¾ cup superfine caster sugar

Place the milk in a saucepan and add the vanilla bean, cut in half lengthwise, or a few drops of vanilla extract, and a pinch of salt. Bring to a boil and then remove from heat. Leave to infuse.

Beat together the egg yolks and sugar until the mixture becomes pale. Remove the vanilla bean from the mix and scrape the insides into the mixture. Gradually whisk the milk into the eggs. Pour the mixture back into the pan and cook over low heat for about 10 minutes, stirring constantly. Do not allow to boil.

Remove pan from heat as soon as the custard is thick enough to coat a spoon; let cool, stirring from time to time to prevent a skin from forming.

Makes 8–10 servings

This light custard sauce is good for everything. Pour it over any fruit; mix it with a raspberry coulis and make a fancy design on your dessert plate; or just eat it right out of the bowl. I love to top a slice of angel food cake with my favorite fruit in season and then ladle some Crème Anglaise over top—it's light and elegant. Maman likes to add a Kirsh, or liqueur, to it.

CHOCOLATE SOUFFLÉ

4 tablespoons butter, divided

2 tablespoons sugar

2 tablespoons cold water

¾ cup chocolate chips or bittersweet chips (Fair Trade)

4 free-range egg yolks

1 cup sifted powdered sugar

5 free-range egg whites, room temperature

½ teaspoon cream of tartar

Preheat oven to 400 degrees F.

Grease a 6-inch soufflé dish with 2 tablespoons butter; coat inside with sugar, shaking out excess.

Combine the cold water and chocolate chips in the top of a double boiler. Place over hot water until chocolate chips are melted; beat with wire whisk until blended.

Add small pieces of remaining butter to chocolate, 1 piece at a time, beating until butter is melted; cool slightly.

Place egg yolks in a large mixing bowl; beat with an electric mixer until mixture is lemon colored. Add powdered sugar gradually; beat until thick. Add one-fourth of the chocolate mixture and beat with a wire whisk until blended. Add remaining chocolate mixture and beat until well mixed.

Beat egg whites and cream of tartar with electric mixer until stiff peaks form. Fold one-fourth of the egg white mixture into chocolate mixture; blend well. Gently fold in remaining egg white mixture until well mixed. Spoon into prepared soufflé dish and smooth top. Bake 35 minutes, or until set. Dust with additional powdered sugar and serve immediately.

Makes 6 servings

GATEAU BRETON

4 cups flour

2 cups sugar

2 cups salted butter, softened

8 free-range egg yolks, 1 yolk
   reserved for glazing top

2 tablespoons rum

2 tablespoons organic milk

Preheat oven to 390 degrees F.

Sift the flour and make a hole in the middle. Add sugar and butter and mix together. Stir in egg yolks and then add rum. Work to a smooth dough. Grease a springform pan with butter, dust with flour, and press the dough evenly into the pan. Mix the remaining egg yolk with the milk, coat the surface of the dough with it, and score a grid pattern with a fork. Bake 45 minutes; cool in pan.

Makes 10 servings

SPRITZ COOKIES

1 cup soft butter
⅔ cup sugar
3 free-range egg yolks
1 teaspoon flavoring (almond
    or vanilla)
2½ cups flour
Food coloring (optional)

Preheat oven to 400 degrees F.

Mix together all ingredients except flour and food coloring.

Work the flour in with a spoon.

Add food coloring as desired to make them seasonal. Force the dough through a cookie press onto an ungreased baking sheet in shapes (letters, rosettes, wreaths, etc.). Bake 7 to 10 minutes until set but not brown.

Makes 6 dozen cookies

Every year my friend Eileen would have a Christmas cookie exchange party. My kids loved that day; I'd come home with 6 to 10 dozen different homemade cookies from all the ladies that came to the party. It sometimes seemed like one more chore, one more thing to do in the middle of the holiday season, but once I started cooking and arrived at Eileen's festive exchange, I remembered what the holidays were all about. Catching up with friends, sharing stories of our children, and, best of all, getting at least a dozen of Eileen's famous Spritz Cookies. My son, Tommy, would eat them all. They were little green wreath cookies with red bow icing—all the same, all bite size, all delectable. In memory of Eileen, start your own cookie exchange. It is soooo fun.

VANILLA SOUFFLÉ

2 cups organic milk

½ cup sugar

½ vanilla pod or 1 teaspoon
   vanilla extract

¼ cup butter

⅓ cup all-purpose flour

6 free-range egg whites, stiffly
   beaten

Combine the milk, sugar, and vanilla pod, if using, in a small heavy saucepan; bring to a boil. Add vanilla extract, if using, and then remove saucepan from heat and let stand 30 minutes. Remove vanilla pod and dry and store for future use.

Melt butter in a double boiler over medium heat. Stir in flour to make a smooth paste using a wooden spoon. Add milk mixture gradually, stirring constantly; cook until thickened. Pour into large mixing bowl; cool slightly. Thoroughly fold in one-fourth of the egg whites using a wire whisk. Add remaining egg whites; fold in thoroughly. Pour into a well-buttered 6- or 7-inch soufflé dish. Smooth top and dome mixture slightly in center. Bake in a preheated oven at 425 degrees F one shelf above center for 25 minutes, or a little longer for a drier soufflé. Serve immediately.

Makes 4 servings

DESSERT CRÊPES

2 cups flour

1/8 teaspoon salt

3 tablespoons sugar

2 cups organic milk, divided

3 free-range eggs, yolks and
    whites separated

1/8 teaspoon vanilla or 2 table-
    spoons rum or cognac

3 tablespoons butter, divided

1/3 cup water

This batter should be made in advance and allowed to stand at least 15 minutes before it is used.

Mix together the flour, salt, and sugar. Moisten flour with 1/2 cup milk. Add the egg yolks and the slightly beaten whites; add vanilla or liqueur and 2 tablespoons melted butter. Mix the rest of the milk with the water and then add the liquid to the mixture. Let rest a while.

Grease a hot skillet, 8 to 9 inches in diameter, with remaining butter. Pour a small amount of batter into the skillet, just enough to cover the bottom of the pan. Swirl batter in pan to spread evenly. Brown on the underside and then turn and brown the other side. When crêpes are ready to turn, bubbles form on top and the sides are brown. Stack crêpes on an ovenware plate and keep warm. To serve, fold as shown in the picture or roll like a cigar. Eat them with fresh strawberries and cream, powdered sugar and lemon juice, Nutella, or anything you desire.

Makes 4 servings

CHOCOLATE CAKE
WITH PRALINE LAVA

¾ cup butter

1 cup semisweet chocolate pieces

3 free-range eggs

3 free-range egg yolks

⅓ cup sugar

1½ teaspoons vanilla

⅓ cup all-purpose flour

3 teaspoons unsweetened cocoa powder

⅓ cup pecan halves, toasted

PRALINE LAVA

½ cup granulated sugar

⅓ cup packed brown sugar

2 tablespoons dark-colored corn syrup

½ cup whipping cream

Preheat oven to 400 degrees F.

Lightly grease and flour six 1- to 1¼-cup ramekins. Place dishes in a shallow baking pan and set pan aside.

In a heavy small saucepan, melt butter and semisweet chocolate over low heat, stirring constantly. Remove from heat; cool.

Meanwhile prepare Praline Lava (see instructions below); cover and keep warm until needed.

Beat eggs, egg yolks, sugar, and vanilla in a large mixing bowl with an electric mixer on high speed for 5 minutes, or until thick and lemon colored. Beat in cooled chocolate mixture on medium speed. Sift flour and cocoa powder over chocolate mixture; beat on low speed just until combined. Divide batter evenly into prepared dishes or cups. Bake 10 minutes.

Pull cakes from oven. Using a small spatula or table knife, puncture top of each partially baked cake and gently enlarge to make a dime-size hole. Slowly spoon about 1 tablespoon Praline Lava into center of each cake. Return to oven. Bake 5 minutes more, or until cakes feel firm around the edges. Cool cakes in dishes on a wire rack for 3 minutes. Using a knife, loosen cakes from sides of dishes and slip out, upright, onto individual dessert plates. Stir toasted pecan halves into the remaining Praline Lava. If necessary, stir 1 to 2 teaspoons of hot water into remaining sauce to thin. Spoon warm Praline Lava on top of cakes. Serve immediately.

To make the lava, combine the sugars and corn syrup in a heavy medium-size saucepan. Stir in cream. Cook over medium-high heat until mixture boils, stirring constantly to dissolve sugar; reduce heat. Cook uncovered for 10 minutes, or until thickened, stirring occasionally.

Makes 6 servings

CHOCOLATE PUDDING CAKE

½ cup sugar

¼ cup cocoa

½ cup boiling water

½ teaspoon vanilla

CAKE

½ cup sugar

¼ cup vegetable oil

1 free-range egg

½ cup organic milk

½ teaspoon vanilla

1 cup flour

½ teaspoon salt

1 teaspoon baking powder

1 unbaked pie shell

To make the syrup, mix together all ingredients and set aside.

To make the cake, cream together the sugar, oil, and egg; set aside.

Mix together remaining ingredients except the pie shell and add to cream mixture. Pour cake mixture into pie shell and then add syrup mixture on top.

Bake at 375 degrees F for 45 to 50 minutes. Don't over bake; it's supposed to be gooey inside.

Makes 4–6 servings

GRANDMA OLGA JEANNE'S CARROT CAKE

CAKE

2 cups flour

2 teaspoons baking powder

1½ teaspoons baking soda

1½ teaspoons cinnamon

2 cups brown sugar

1½ cups oil

4 eggs

2 cups grated organic carrots

1 cup drained crushed
   pineapple (optional)

½ cup pecans

ICING

½ cup butter, softened

8 ounces cream cheese,
   softened

1 teaspoon vanilla

Date sugar, to taste

Preheat oven to 350 degrees F.

Sift together the flour, baking powder, baking soda, and cinnamon. Add the sugar, oil, and eggs; mix well. Stir in the carrots, pineapple, and nuts. Pour batter into a lightly greased 9 x 13-inch pan and bake for 35–40 minutes, or until done in the center. Let cool completely on a wire rack.

To make the icing, combine the butter, cream cheese, and vanilla. Add sugar slowly until desired consistency is reached. If icing is too thick, add a little milk to thin. Frost cooled cake and serve. Dennis and Sandy Dierks contributed this delicious recipe.

Makes 8–10 servings

LEMON CHEESECAKE
WITH GINGERSNAP CRUST

CRUST

20 vanilla wafer cookies

10 gingersnap cookies

3 tablespoons sugar

1 tablespoon grated lemon peel

1/4 cup unsalted butter, melted

FILLING

1 tablespoon plus 3/4 teaspoon
   unflavored gelatin

1/4 cup cold water

Zest from 2 lemons, removed
   with vegetable peeler

1 (1-inch) piece fresh ginger,
   peeled

3/4 generous cup sugar

2 tablespoons plus a pinch
   of salt

3 large free-range egg yolks

3/4 cup organic milk (no low-fat
   or nonfat)

12 ounces cream cheese, room
   temperature

1/3 cup fresh lemon juice

1 1/2 cups chilled whipping
   cream

Lemon Curd (see facing page)

Fresh mint sprigs

Place rack in center of oven and preheat oven to 350 degrees F.

To make the crust, lightly oil a 9-inch round pie pan. Finely grind vanilla wafers, gingersnaps, sugar, and lemon peel in a food processor. Add butter and blend well. Sprinkle crumbs over bottom of prepared pan; press to form bottom crust. Bake 12 minutes, or until golden brown; cool.

To make the filling, sprinkle gelatin over cold water in a small bowl. Let stand 10 minutes to soften. Mince lemon peel and ginger with sugar and salt in food processor until lemon peel and ginger are as fine as sugar. Add yolks and blend until light and fluffy. Scald milk in a heavy saucepan. With processor running, add milk through feed tube and blend well. Return mixture to saucepan. Stir over medium-low heat until mixture thickens and leaves a path on back of a spoon when finger is drawn across, about 12 minutes; do not boil. Add gelatin mixture to custard and stir until dissolved. Strain into bowl, pressing on solids with back of spoon. Refrigerate 20 minutes, or until thickened but not set, stirring often.

Blend the cream cheese and lemon juice in food processor until smooth. Add custard and blend until smooth. Pour into a large bowl. Whip the cream in a medium bowl to soft peaks. Gently fold into filling. Pour half of filling over crust. Spoon half of Lemon Curd by tablespoonfuls over filling. Swirl mixtures together using tip of knife. Pour remaining filling over top. Spoon remaining curd over by tablespoonfuls. Swirl mixtures together using tip of knife. Refrigerate cheesecake at least 4 hours or overnight. Garnish with mint.

Makes 12 servings

LEMON CURD

¼ teaspoon unflavored gelatin

1 teaspoon water

1 tablespoon grated lemon peel

½ cup sugar

¼ cup fresh lemon juice

3 large free-range egg yolks

6 tablespoons unsalted butter

Sprinkle gelatin over water in a small cup. Let stand 10 minutes to soften. Mince lemon peel with sugar in a processor until it is as fine as sugar. Transfer to a small heavy saucepan. Mix in lemon juice and yolks and then add the butter. Stir over medium heat until very thick, about 5 minutes; do not boil. Pour into a bowl. Add gelatin and stir to dissolve. Cool completely, stirring frequently, about 1 hour. Serve on ice cream, toast, or with fresh strawberries.

Makes 1 cup

INDUSTRIALIZED CONVENTIONAL VS. LOCAL SUSTAINABLE AGRICULTURE

It's time we stop guessing where our meat comes from, what's in our milk, and how our strawberries got so big. This is not a push for you to become a vegetarian or a vegan. My intention is not to condemn or ostracize the eater of conventionally grown food. Regardless of how committed we are to eating local, seasonal, and organic, to some extent we have all been a part of creating this fast food–nation. Fortunately, we, as a community of eaters, have the opportunity to create an alternative system, to demand food that embodies our values and that is founded on transparency, honesty, and respect.

Over the course of this chapter, I have taken a snapshot look at the production of six foods—beef, dairy, chicken, eggs, strawberries, and leafy greens—and offered more sustainable, life-affirming alternatives. Consider this an introduction to the issues, as it's nearly impossible to summarize the complete picture in a matter of pages.

My hope is that this glimpse will encourage you to embark on your own exploration of your food system. Following this chapter is a list of books that will help you flush out the issues I address and much more. I invite you to become an educated eater and to vote for a food system that we can be proud of; one that we can pass on to our children with a clear conscience.

BEEF: MORE SUSTAINABLE ALTERNATIVES

Concentrated (or Confined) Animal Feeding Operations (CAFOs) are agricultural facilities that house and feed a large number of animals in a confined area for forty-five days or more during any twelve-month period. Large CAFOs are defined by the U.S. Environmental Protection Agency as livestock operations that contain more than one thousand beef cattle, though some feedlots in the central plains may hold up to one hundred thousand animals.[1]

There are many emerging alternatives to the conventional CAFO model of beef production, including many local ranches that are opting out of the CAFO circuit, keeping their herd at home, and seeking direct marketing opportunities.

The environmental benefits of carefully managed pasture-based systems are potentially significant. It has been predicted that the adoption of pasture systems would reduce emissions of greenhouse gases by 40 percent, decrease soil erosion by 50 to 80 percent, decrease fuel use, and improve water quality. This study also demonstrated the benefits of carbon sequestration, less soil nutrient loss, and decreased sediment in waterways.[2] Restored pasture lands make good homes for both cattle and diverse populations of insects and wild animals.

Good management of pastures and adjacent riparian areas (water edges) can offer these environmental benefits and more, while improving the living conditions of the animals and simultaneously benefiting the producer's triple bottom line.

LESS MEAN, MORE LEAN

Meat from a grass-fed steer is leaner and has less marbling, with about one-half to one-third the fat as a comparable cut from a grain-fed animal. Lower in calories, grass-fed beef is also higher in vitamin E and omega-3 fatty acids, which are thought to help reduce the risk of cancer, lower the likelihood of high blood pressure, and make people less susceptible to depression. Furthermore, meat from grass-fed cattle is rich in conjugated linoleic acid (CLA), another beneficial fat, which supposedly lowers the risk of cancer.[3]

I'd like to interject that when I was growing up, meat was reserved for special occasions and portions were small. This was typical practice for most Americans, and we were healthier for it. But when beef production became wildly industrialized and meat prices became more affordable for everyday consumption, meat moved to the center of the plate rather than the side. Although organic pastured beef is a healthier product on multiple levels, it would still be wise to pare back our consumption and simply choose quality over quantity.

HARVESTED MEAT

Even the language of the slaughter is different outside the CAFO jungle. Many of our local ranchers describe the process of preparing their animals for market as "harvesting." The process is slower and more controlled than in a CAFO. Great care is taken to ensure that the animal is as relaxed as possible. It is an act of reverence. At Prather Ranch, one of the first certified-organic and certified-humane operations in Northern California, there is a plaque that rests above the space where cows are downed; it reads, "Take a moment, you're about to take a life."

THE LABELS

While there is room for improvement on the transparency front when it comes to helping the customer navigate the new list of labels, including natural, grass-fed, pastured, certified organic, and certified humane, the shift toward a production system that is better for the animal, better for the land, better for the rancher, and better for the eater is exciting and well overdue. First, here's a little help on those labels as they relate to beef.

- **Certified Humane:** To meet USDA organic standards, cattle must be raised under organic management for the last third of gestation, be fed 100-percent organic agricultural feed products, whether grass or grain, be free of antibiotics and growth hormones, and be given access to pasture (though for indeterminate amounts of time).[4]

- **Certified Humane:** In response to the fact that USDA organic regulations do not specifically address the living conditions of animals, a team of veterinarians and animal scientists developed the Certified Humane Animal Care Standards. The standards require producers to allow animals to engage in their natural behavior; raise animals with sufficient space, shelter, and gentle handling to limit stress; and ensure that animals have ample fresh water and a healthy diet without added antibiotics or hormones. Participating businesses must undergo rigorous inspections before they can use the Certified Humane label to market their products.[5]
- **Natural:** The USDA defines natural as a product containing no artificial ingredient or added color and is only minimally processed. The label must explain the use of the term natural (such as no added colorings or artificial ingredients; minimally processed). The claim "natural" is otherwise unregulated, and does not require a certification process.
- **Free-range:** Free-range implies that animals are not confined and have access to roam pasture freely. There are no USDA certifications that regulate "free-range" livestock.
- **Grass-fed:** Beef that is grass-fed has been raised primarily on a natural diet of grasses. Grass-fed cows enjoy a more natural growth trajectory and significantly decrease the ranch's dependency on subsidized grain. Still, some ranchers that market their beef as grass-fed occasionally supplement their herd's diet with grain when local grasses are dry. There are no USDA certifications that regulate what percentage of the animal's diet is grass, nor how often the herd is out grazing open fields.
- **Pastured:** Pastured livestock forage for their meals on pasture, a system that allows cows the opportunity "to express their true cow-ness," in the words of revolutionary "grass-farmer" Joel Salatin of Polyface Farm. In the most "intensive" models, such as managed intensive rotational grazing, cows eat forage only, move to a new pasture paddock roughly every day, and stay herded tightly with portable electric fencing. This natural model heals the land, thickens the forage, reduces weeds, stimulates earthworms, reduces pathogens, and increases nutritional qualities in the meat.[6] There are no USDA certifications that regulate pastured livestock.

NO ANTIBIOTICS

USDA Organic regulations prohibit the use of antibiotics. Fortunately the combination of more natural diets and more sanitary living conditions translate to healthier cows. In the case that a cow does fall ill and antibiotics must be administered, the cow is pulled from production line until the antibiotics are guaranteed to have left the cow's system.

USDA Organic regulations prohibit the use of growth hormones. Without these inputs, cows develop at a slower, more natural rate. Eaters can rest assured that hormone residuals won't be found in their beef nor polluting local waterways.

DAIRY: MORE SUSTAINABLE ALTERNATIVES

While the average dairy cow produced more than five thousand pounds of milk a year in 1950, today's average factory-farmed cow produces more than eighteen thousand pounds a year, thanks to grain-based diets,[4] growth hormones, and increased exposure to light.

The USDA requires dairy animals to be managed organically for at least twelve months in order for dairy products to be labeled and sold as organic. Like organic beef herds, dairy herds must be given 100-percent organic feed, be free of antibiotics and growth hormones, and must have access to pasture, although for indeterminate amounts of time.

Studies have found that milk from organically raised dairy cows is on average 50 percent higher in Vitamin E than conventionally produced milk; is 75 percent higher in beta carotene, which the body converts into Vitamin A; is two to three times higher in select antioxidants; and displays higher levels of omega-3 essential fatty acids and CLA.[1] If nutritional value isn't compelling enough, trust your taste buds. Many milk drinkers claim that organic milk, especially from pastured cows, simply tastes better.

In the spirit of transparency, it's important to acknowledge that even some organic dairies are raising cows in less than dreamy bucolic conditions. For example, Horizon and Aurora, the nation's two largest mega-dairies, have been criticized for not providing animals with adequate pasture time and for having CAFO-size herds. As a result, Aurora recently reduced one of its Colorado dairies from more than four thousand cows to one thousand! While organic certification is a good step in the right direction, consumer demand for transparent practices, supported by a willingness to pay a fair price for quality products, are pivotal to realizing truly healthy, viable food systems.

COOPERATIVES AND NICHE MARKETS

Across the country, there are a growing number of dairies bucking the trend toward CAFO operations. Owners of small-scale dairies are thinking creatively about how they can run a viable competitive business and still maintain the environmental and ethical values of their farm. Some of these alternative avenues include farm cooperatives and niche marketing, for example:

Organic Valley is a countrywide cooperative of more than twelve hundred small family farms that share a mission of environmental sustainability. Within "the un-corporation," all of its member farmers have a say in how the business is run and benefit from coming together under one label in a profit-sharing agreement. This business model enables them to survive in the face of large corporate competitors and benefits both the consumer and the farmer—consumers receive quality organic products at fair prices and regional family farms earn livable wages.

My favorite dairy of all time, Straus Family Creamery, became the first certified organic dairy in California in 1994. Whether it's sending their milk to market in glass containers, generating 95 percent of their farm's energy from their herd's manure via a methane digester, milling their own organic grain to supplement the herd's diet during the dry months, or talking about acre to cow ratios rather than cow to acre (their three hundred cows graze 668 acres in Marin and Sonoma counties), Straus Family Creamery remains on the forefront of the organic dairy niche.[2] They provide us with this quality milk knowing that their limited production cannot compete with mainstream brands. Straus Family Creamery milk may cost a little more then the average grocery store milk, but I'm worth it and so are you. Make your food choices healthy choices.

RBGH-FREE

Today, the European Union, Japan, Australia, and Canada have all banned the use of the artificial protein hormone rBGH (Bovine Growth Hormone) due to health concerns for animals and humans alike. Many U.S. dairies, both organic and conventional, have elected to raise their herds without the use of rBGH, believing that a system free of artificial hormones is better for their customers, their animals, and their land. A growing community of food suppliers is listening to consumer demand: grocery chains Kroger and Safeway banned rBGH milk in their store-brand dairy products in 2007, Starbucks discontinued their use of rBGH milk in January 2008, and Wal-Mart banned rBGH milk in their store-brand dairy products in March 2008.

Of course, where there is change, one can expect to find resistance. In this case it stems from the agricultural company Monsanto, maker of rBGH, which has sued a number of dairies for using rBGH-free labels. The FDA, requires rBGH-free dairy products to list the following disclaimer "no significant difference has been shown between milk derived from rBGH-supplemented and non-rBGH-supplemented cows." We'll leave that up to the informed milk-drinker to decide.

CHICKEN: MORE SUSTAINABLE ALTERNATIVES

Conventional broiler chickens are raised in sheds, which typically hold up to twenty thousand chickens, approximately 130 square inches per bird.[3] Chickens require at least 291 square inches of personal space to flap their wings.[4]

In addition to enjoying a more humane

and natural life, pasture-raised chickens are significantly higher in omega-3 fatty acids, CLA, beta-carotenes, and Vitamin A than conventionally raised broilers.[1]

ORGANIC

The USDA requires that certified-organic chickens be raised under organic management, no later than the second day of life. They must be given 100-percent organic feed and have access to the outdoors, although for indeterminate amounts of time. They are not to be given antibiotics.

FREE-RANGE

While there is no specific USDA certification process to validate the free-range label, it is assumed within the organic certification that chickens have access to the outdoors. Many free-range operations have been criticized for providing just slightly better living conditions than conventional grower houses, with just a little more space per chicken and small doors leading outside, which chickens rarely venture through. Still, the demand for organic and free-range chicken is increasing as people become more aware of the conditions of grower houses. As that demand increases, so will the transparency of free-range.

PASTURED CHICKENS

While there is no specific USDA certification for pastured chickens, there are a growing number of ranches that are raising chickens that are free

to express their true nature. Flocks are much smaller and are allowed to forage on pasture. One of our local ranchers, David Evans of Marin Sun Farms, uses 12 x 12 x 2.5 feet floorless portable field shelters to move 75 birds to a fresh paddock of pasture daily. Under such conditions, the birds benefit from fresh air, exercise, sunshine, and a diverse diet of natural grub.[2]

EGGS: MORE SUSTAINABLE ALTERNATIVES

Nearly three hundred forty million factory-farmed egg-laying hens in the United States are confined to wired battery cages. Fortunately, alternatives are hatching.

Visit the egg section at your local grocery store, and if you're lucky enough to peruse dozens of alternatives to conventionally produced eggs, chances are you'll be encouraged and then you might start to feel a bit confused. You're not alone. Antibiotic-free, cage-free, certified-organic, farm-fresh, free-range, and pastured are just some of the labels we find on egg cartons these days, many of which paint a lovely pastoral image of where our eggs were presumably laid. Navigating the marketing maze is the first step to finding the alternative that matches your values. Again, here's a little help with the labels.

THE LABELS

- **Certified Organic:** The USDA requires that certified organic eggs come from chickens that are raised under organic management, fed 100-percent organic feed, free of antibiotics, and have access to the outdoors for indeterminate amounts of time.[1] Often accompanying the organic certification are *antibiotic-free*, *cage-free*, and *free-range*. These can be assumed, given the product's organic certification, though the conscious consumer may want to dig a little deeper.

- **Antibiotic-Free:** Implies that the hens were raised without antibiotics. Apart from organic certification, antibiotic-free claims are on the honor system.
- **Cage-Free:** Cage-free implies that the hens were not raised in cages but free to roam about a defined area. For the vast majority of flocks, this means that birds are raised in still rather confined warehouse-type structures. Apart from organic certification, cage-free claims are on the honor system. We're making progress, but we've still got a long way to go.
- **Free-Range:** This is one of the most widely used and most confusing messages for the eater to decipher, especially when paired with pastoral images on egg carton labels. Free-range implies that the birds have access to the outdoors (this is the extent to which the USDA defines free-range). However, like broiler chicken operations, many egg operations have been criticized for misrepresenting how freely their chickens roam. Many farms have small doors on the sides of their barns which

meet the organic standards but through which the chickens never venture. Apart from organic certification, free-range claims are on the honor system. Again, this is another opportunity for the consumer to demand a more transparent system.

- **Farm-Fresh:** Implies that eggs are fresh from the farm. Like most all foods, the freshest eggs are the ones that change hands the least. Buying direct from a farmer at the farmers market is your best opportunity to find true farm-fresh eggs, unless you have some backyard chickens.
- **Pastured:** Pastured eggs come from hens that have been raised on pasture. While there is no specific USDA certification for pastured hens, there is a growing number of ranches raising hens and collecting eggs in a truly pastoral setting. Marin Sun Farms houses their pastured hens in a movable coop, complete with boxes lined with bedding, an elevated floor, and a roost. The chicken coops are moved daily, following the trail of pastured cows. The chickens are accustomed to spending their days foraging about the coop and then moving inside for the night.[2] It is a mutually beneficial system. The chickens benefit from a diet of tender fresh shoots of grass and bugs that are hatching in the cow manure. The pasture benefits from the chickens breaking up the cow pies, eating the bugs, and depositing their own fertilizers, ultimately enriching the soil before moving on to the next pasture.

Free from battery cages, beak clipping, and artificial lighting, laying hens live healthier lives within these more sustainable systems and even produce eggs that are more nutrient-rich. In a recent egg-testing project conducted by *Mother Earth News,* eggs from pastured hens contained one-third less cholesterol, one-fourth less saturated fat, two-thirds more vitamin A, two times the omega-3 fatty acids, three times more vitamin E, and seven times more beta carotene compared to USDA nutrient data for commercial eggs.[3] The nutritional superiority of these eggs makes it easier to justify spending a few extra dollars—especially when you can be certain the growing conditions are humane and environmentally sound. If there's any lingering confusion, ask your farmer, visit a farm, and demand transparency.

STRAWBERRIES: MORE SUSTAINABLE ALTERNATIVES

Conventionally grown strawberries are one of the most chemically intensive fruits produced.

Strawberries can be produced more safely and more efficiently by using organic practices, such as incorporating integrated pest management (using beneficial insects to manage harmful ones) and planting cover crops, which create a more bio-diverse environment, disorienting potentially destructive bugs.

Organic strawberry production eliminates the use of toxic chemicals, like methyl bromide, something that world leaders have been trying to do since 1992. While both conventional and organic systems return less energy in harvestable products than in the amount of energy embodied in the inputs, more than 43 percent of energy inputs for an organic system are from renewable sources compared to only 2 percent in conventional systems. Because organic strawberry yields are on average 25 percent lower than conventional systems, the price attached tends to be higher.[1] But don't be fooled by the affordability of conventional strawberries, the hidden cost of the conventional system's dependency on methyl bromide is not something we should take lightly.

LEAFY GREENS: MORE SUSTAINABLE ALTERNATIVES

In September 2006, while it seemed as though the entire country was turned upside down over the safety of its conventionally grown bagged greens and yet another e.coli scare, my husband and I were eating fresh spinach and salad mix without even an inkling of fear. I have the good fortune of knowing where my greens come from, and with that comes a confidence in their safety. Dennis Dierks of Paradise Valley Produce brings them fresh to the market from his ten-acre farm in Bolinas, where he has been growing organic greens and vegetables for more than thirty years. He is one of those back-to-the-land hippies that I fondly referred to while

Dennis and Sandy Dierks of Paradise Valley Farm in Bolinas.

recounting the history of farmers markets.

Dennis and his wife, Sandy, didn't have experience with farming when they started, but they learned quickly. Instead of getting big, they went deep, delving into organic, biodynamic, and microbial agriculture. This is where they lose me, I just trust their lettuce is safe. Their goal is to create a truly sustainable food system, gathering all of the nutrients that they use on

their farm from within five miles of their land. Whereas the farms of Salinas, California, "the Salad Bowl of the World," got swept into fulfilling the nation-wide demand for fresh vibrant organic greens, the Dierks are fulfilling that niche in their local community. Dennis and Sandy reflect that growing food has been a fulfilling experience for their entire family. It has been an equally fulfilling experience for my family to enjoy all the freshness, flavor, and embodied positive energy of the Dierks' food.

SUGGESTED READING LIST

This list covers the gamut, from food to water to economics to the emerging sustainability movement—as the forces behind the local food movement are diverse and intimately interconnected. I hope you'll find them helpful along your path to becoming not just a more conscious eater but also a more conscious citizen.

Animal, Vegetable, Miracle: A Year of Food Life by Barbara Kingsolver, Camille Kingsolver, and Steven L. Hopp

Appetite For Profit: How the Food Industry Undermines Our Health and How to Fight Back by Michele Simon

Biomimicry: Innovation Inspired by Nature by Janine M. Benyus

Blessed Unrest: How the Largest Social Movement in History is Restoring Grace, Justice, and Beauty to the World by Paul Hawken

Cadillac Desert: The American West and Its Disappearing Water by Marc Reisner

Cradle to Cradle: Remaking the Way We Make Things by William McDonough and Michael Braungart

Deep Economy: The Wealth of Communities and the Durable Future by Bill McKibben

Epitaph for a Peach: Four Seasons on My Family Farm by David Masumoto

Everything I Want to Do is Illegal: War Stories for the Local Food Front by Joel Salatin

Fast Food Nation by Eric Schlosser

Food Fight: The Citizen's Guide to a Food and Farm Bill by Daniel Imhoff

Food Politics: How the Food Industry Influences Nutrition, and Health by Marion Nestle

In Defense of Food: An Eater's Manifesto by Michael Pollan

Natural Capital: Creating the Next Industrial Revolution by Paul Hawken, Amory Lovins, and L. Hunter Lovins

Slow Food Nation: Why Our Food Should Be Good, Clean and Fair by Carlo Petrini

The Omnivore's Dilemma: A Natural History of Four Meals by Michael Pollan

The Revolution Will Not Be Microwaved: Inside America's Underground Food Movements by Sandor Ellix Katz

The Unsetting of America: Culture & Agriculture by Wendel Berry

What to Eat by Marion Nestle

SUGGESTED FILMS

An Inconvenient Truth
King Corn: You Are What You Eat
Super Size Me
The 11th Hour
The Future of Food
The Real Dirt on Farmer John

NOTES

INTRODUCTION: A FRENCH-AMERICAN PARADOX

1 Wendell Berry, "Nation's Destructive Farm Policy Is Everyone's Concern," July 11, 1999, http://www.agrecon.mcgill.ca/ecoagr/doc/berry.htm (accessed August 19, 2008).

HOW TO SAVE THE WORLD ONE RECIPE AT A TIME

1 Matthew Hora and Jody Tick, *From Farm to Table: Making the Connection in the Mid-Atlantic Food System* (Washington DC: Capital Area Food Bank, 2001).

2 Slow Food, http://www.slowfood.com/about_us/eng/philosophy.lasso (accessed May 30, 2008).

3 United States Department of Agriculture, "Cooperative State Research, Education, and Extension Service," http://www.csrees.usda.gov/qlinks/extension.html (accessed April 18, 2008).

4 Ibid.

5 United States Department of Agriculture, National Agricultural Statistics Services, 1997 Census of Agriculture, "Farm Acreage, Number and Acres per Farm, 1940–97," http://aic.ucdavis.edu/pubs/I.3.pdf.

6 Zoe Bradbury, "No Farmers? No Food," post to Grist: Environmental News & Commentary, May 20, 2008, http://gristmill.grist.org/story/2008/5/19/8032/52484?source=friend

7 Global Footprint Network, "Ecological Footprint: Overview," http://www.footprintnetwork.org/gfn_sub.php?content=footprint_overview (accessed May 30, 2007). Also visit http://www.footprintnetwork.org/gfn_sub.php?content=myfootprint to calculate how many earths it would take to support your lifestyle if everyone lived like you. Notice that your food choices are one of the primary factors in calculating your global footprint.

8 Leo Horrigan, Robert S. Lawrence, and Polly Walker, "How Sustainable Agriculture Can Address the Environmental and Human Health Harms of Industrial Agriculture," *Environmental Health Perspectives* 110, no. 5 (May 2002): 446.

9 Ibid.

10 Ibid.

11 Barbara Kingsolver, *Animal, Vegetable, Miracle* (New York: Harper Collins Publishers, 2007), 5.

IT'S TIME TO LEAVE FAST FOOD AND GO BACK TO SLOW FOOD

1 Trust for America's Heath, "F as in Fat: How Obesity Policies are Failing in America," October 20, 2004, http://healthyamericans.org/reports/obesity/.

2 K. M. Narayan, James P. Boyle, Theodore J. Thompson, Stephen W. Sorenson, and David

F. Williamson, "Lifetime Risk for Diabetes Mellitus in the United States," *Journal of the American Medical Association* 290, no. 14 (2003): 1884–90.

3 Trust for America's Heath, "F as in Fat," http://healthyamericans.org/reports/obesity/.

4 S. Jay Olshansky et al, "A Potential Decline in Life Expectancy in the United States in the 21st Century," The New England Journal of Medicine 352, no. 11 (March 17, 2005): 1138–45.

5 http://www.eurekalert.org/pub_releases/2005-03/ps-sta031805.php) (accessed September 16, 2008).

6 http://www.ces.ncsu.edu/depts/hort/hil/hil-11.html (accessed September 16, 2008).

INDUSTRIALIZED CONVENTIONAL AGRICULTURE VS. LOCAL SUSTAINABLE AGRICULTURE

BEEF

1 U.S. Environmental Protection Agency National Pollutant Discharge Elimination System (NPDES) Glossary, March 2004, http://cfpub.epa.gov/npdes/glossary.cfm#L.

2 George Boody, Bruce Vondracek, David A. Andow, Mara Krinke, John Westra, Julie Zimmerman, and Patrick Welle, "Multifunctional agriculture in the United States," *BioScience* 55, no. 1 (January 2005): 27–38.

3 *PBS Frontline*, "Grass-fed vs. Corn-fed Beef," http://www.pbs.org/wgbh/pages/frontline/shows/meat/safe/know.html (accessed May 30, 2008).

4 United States Department of Agriculture, Agricultural Marketing Service, National Organic Program (NOP), "Organic Production and Handling Standards," April 2008, http://www.ams.usda.gov/AMSv1.0/getfile?dDocName=STELDEV3004445 (accessed July 31, 2008).

5 Certified Humane Raised & Handled, "What is Certified Humane Raised & Handled?" http://www.certifiedhumane.org/whatis.html (accessed May 30, 2008).

6 Polyface, Inc., "Product Descriptions," 2007, http://www.polyfacefarms.com/products.aspx (accessed May 30, 2008).

DAIRY

1 *BBC News*, "Study Shows Organic Milk Contains More Vitamins and Health-Promoting Antioxidants," January 7, 2005, http://www.organicconsumers.org/organic/milk011005.cfm (accessed May 30, 2008).

2 Matthew Green, "Udder Confusion: Difficult Choices in the Dairy Aisle," *Edible East Bay*, spring 2008. Newsletter Web site is www.edibleeastbay.com, but articles are not posted online.

CHICKEN

1 Forks Farm Market, "The Nutritional
Benefits of Foods Raised on Pasture,"
http://www.forksfarmmarket.com/
Downloads/2003NewsLtrArticle.pdf
(accessed May 30, 2008).

2 Marin Sun Farms, http://www.
marinsunfarms.com/our_poultry.html
(accessed May 30, 2008).

EGGS

1 United States Department of Agriculture,
Agricultural Marketing Service, National
Organic Program, October 2002, http://www.
ams.usda.gov/AMSv1.0/getfile?dDocName-
STELDEV3004445 (accessed May 30, 2008).

2 Marin Sun Farms, http://www.
marinsunfarms.com/our_poultry.html
(accessed May 30, 2008).

3 *Mother Earth News*, "Meet Real Free-
Range Eggs," October/November 2007,
http://www.motherearthnews.com/Real-
Food/2007-10-01/Tests-Reveal-Healtheir-
Eggs.aspx (accessed May 30, 2008).

STRAWBERRIES

1 Agroecology, "Organic Versus
Conventional," http://www.agroecology.org/
Case%20Studies/strawberries.html (accessed
September 16, 2008).

RESOURCES

To find any of the farmers or food purveyors celebrated in this book, please visit www.marinfarmersmarkets.org.

SUSTAINABLE AGRICULTURE RESOURCES

Buy Fresh Buy Local Guide,
    http://guide.buylocalca.org

Center for Ecoliteracy, www.ecoliteracy.org

California Certified Organic Farmers,
    www.ccof.org

California Federation of Certified Farmers'
    Markets, www.cafarmersmarkets.com

Community Alliance with Family Farmers,
    www.caff.org

Eat Well Guide, www.eatwellguide.org

Elite Farmer, www.elitefarmer.com

Electronic Benefit Transfer Project (Federal
    Food Stamps),
    http://www.ebtproject.ca.gov/

Farmers Market Coalition,
    www.farmersmarketcoalition.org

Food Declaration, www.fooddeclaration.org

Grown in Marin, www.growninmarin.com

Local Harvest, www.localharvest.org

Locavores, www.locavores.com

Marin Agricultural Land Trust, www.malt.org

Marin Organic, www.marinorganic.org

Roots of Change, www.rocfund.org

Slow Food, www.slowfoodusa.org

Sustainable Agriculture Education,
    www.sagecenter.org

WIC – Farmers Market Nutrition Program,
    www.fns.usda.gov/wic/FMNP/default.htm

FARMERS MARKETS IN THE NORTH BAY

MARIN COUNTY

Marin Farmers Markets
Fairfax Farmers' Market, Wednesday (Seasonal)
Marin Civic Center Farmers' Markets,
    Thursday and Sunday (Year-round)
Novato Farmers' Market, Tuesday (Seasonal)
    Contact: 1.800.897.FARM
    www.marinfarmersmarkets.org

Marin Organic
Pt. Reyes Station Farmers' Market, Saturday
    (Seasonal) Contact: 415.663.9667
    www.marinorganic.org

Golden Gate Farmers Market Association
Corte Madera Farmers' Market, Wednesday
    (Year-round)
Larkspur Landing Farmers' Market, Saturday
    (Seasonal)
Mill Valley Farmers' Market, Tuesday (Seasonal)
Ross Farmers' Market, Thursday (Seasonal)
Sausalito Farmers' Market, Friday (Seasonal)
    Contact: 415.382.7846

MENDOCINO COUNTY

Mendocino County Farmers Market Association
Boonville Farmers' Market, Saturday (Seasonal)
Fort Bragg Farmers' Market, Wednesday
    (Seasonal)
Gualala Farmers' Market, Saturday (Seasonal)
Laytonville Farmers' Market, Monday (Seasonal)
Mendocino Farmers' Market, Friday (Seasonal)
Redwood Valley Farmers' Market, Saturday
    (Seasonal)
Ukiah Farmers' Market, Tuesday & Saturday
    (Seasonal)

Willits Farmers' Market, Thursday (Seasonal)
Contact: 707.964.6718
www.mcfarm.org/

SAN FRANCISCO COUNTY

California Farmers' Markets Association
San Francisco, Crocker Galleria, Thursday
(Year-round)
San Francisco, Parkmerced, Saturday (Seasonal)
Contact: 1.800.806.3276
www.cafarmersmkts.com/

San Francisco Heart of City Farmers' Market,
Wednesday & Sunday (Year-round)
Contact: 415.558.9455

**Center for Urban Education about Sustainable
Agriculture**
The Ferry Plaza Farmers Market, Tuesday
and Saturday (Year-round) Contact:
415.291.3276 www.cuesa.org

Noe Valley Farmers' Market, Saturday
(Year-round) Contact: 415.3248.1332
www.noevalleyfarmersmarket.com

Pacific Coast Farmers Markets
Divisadero Farmers' Market, Sunday
(Year-round)
Fillmore Farmers' Market, Saturday
(Year-round)
Kaiser Permanente San Francisco Farmers'
Market, Wednesday (Year-round)
UCSF Farmers' Market, Wednesday (Seasonal)
Contact: 800.949.FARM www.pcfma.com

San Francisco Environment
San Francisco Bayview Hunters Point
Contact: 415.355.3723
www.sfenvironment.org

SONOMA COUNTY

Cotati Farmers' Market, Thursday (Seasonal)
Contact: 707.795.5508

Duncan Mills Farmers' Market, Saturday
(Seasonal) Contact: 707.865.4171

Guerneville Farmers' Market, Tuesday (Seasonal)
Contact: 707.865.4171

Healdsburg Farmers' Market, Tuesday &
Saturday (Seasonal) Contact: 707.431.1956
www.healdsburgfarmersmarket.org

Occidental Farmers' Market, Friday (Seasonal)
Contact: 707.793.2159
www.occidentalfarmersmarket.com

Petaluma Farmers' Market, Saturday (Seasonal)
Contact: 707.524.2123
www.petalumafarmersmarket.com

Santa Rosa Farmers' Market, Wednesday
(Seasonal) www.srdowntownmarket.com

Santa Rosa Farmers' Market, Wednesday
& Saturday (Year-round)
Contact: 707.522.8629

Sebastopol Farmers' Market, Sunday (Seasonal)
Contact: 707.522.9305

Sonoma Farmers' Market, Tuesday (Seasonal) &
Friday (Year-round) Contact: 707.538.7023

Windsor Farmers' Market, Thursday & Sunday
(Seasonal) Contact: 707.433.4595
www.windsorfarmersmarket.com

ACKNOWLEDGMENTS

Thanks to Gibbs Smith for encouraging me and giving me this opportunity—for taking a chance on someone who had never written a book nor wanted to. I'm glad I did. To Katie Newbold, my editor, whose patience and guidance have brought us to a finished product. To Scott, my photographer, and Pouke, my food stylist, who withstood 105 degrees. Thank you.

To Gladys Gilliland, my bluebird leader, for having faith in me. To Jake Ours for being a great mentor. To the San Rafael BID and San Rafael City Council for letting me start their market twenty years ago with no experience. To Bob Berner, Elizabeth, Constance, and the rest of the MALT team for continuing to save the land we hold so dear. Thank you for staying the course. To Steve Quirt for all his enthusiasm and zest for life and farmers. To Ellie Rilla for her life's dedication to Marin Agriculture. To Dominic Grossi for supporting our efforts in building a permanent home for the farmers and heading up the Marin Farm Bureau. To Helge Hellberg of Marin Organic and his team for teaching us how to celebrate around a table filled with local foods. To Stacy Carlson, our Agricultural Commissioner, for being so far ahead of his time with one of the first organic certifying counties in the country. To the Marin County Supervisors for supporting agriculture through twenty-five years of farmers markets, land use, food policies, and friendship. To all the farmers, bakers, food purveyors, and artisans for whom I work. Thank you for letting me do what I love and for being part of my life. To every person I interviewed, thank you for sharing your stories and your food. To Mary Joe for understanding.

To all the team at Marin Farmers Markets and Marin Agricultural Institute, you are the best of the best.

To Maman for teaching me by example that I could do anything if I put my mind to it. I love you. To Papa for teaching me *le joie de vivre*. I love you. To my brothers Roland and Marc, stop fighting. I love you both. To all my family here and in France, I miss you.

To Marie for teaching me how to flip a crêpe. To my cousins Marinette and Juliette for all their love and support these past forty-six years. To Madge, my mother-in-law, who welcomed me with open arms to her family and American dinner table. To my best friend, Patti, for everything.

To my high school sweetheart, Herbie, without whom I wouldn't make it through each day. Thank you for your ever-present love and support. To my three beautiful children, Monique, Liza, and Tommy, and their spouses Chris and Shayla. You are the light of my life. And to the four grandchildren you've blessed me with—Lucq, Ella, Owen, and Tait. Thank you for keeping me young.

And to Amelia. Without your help, this book would not exist. Your passion for a local economy, your smile no matter what we were up against, and your ability to capture the story made it a ride I'd go on again. Thanks partner.

INDEX